Cloud-Based
RDF Data Management

Synthesis Lectures on Data Management

Editor
H.V. Jagadish, *University of Michigan*

Founding Editor
M. Tamer Özsu, *University of Waterloo*

Synthesis Lectures on Data Management is edited by H.V. Jagadish of the University of Michigan. The series publishes 80–150 page publications on topics pertaining to data management. Topics include query languages, database system architectures, transaction management, data warehousing, XML and databases, data stream systems, wide scale data distribution, multimedia data management, data mining, and related subjects.

Cloud-Based RDF Data Management
Zoi Kaoudi, Ioana Manolescu, and Stamatis Zampetakis
2020

Community Search over Big Graphs
Xin Huang, Laks V.S. Lakshmanan, and Jianliang Xu
2019

On Transactional Concurrency Control
Goetz Graefe
2019

Data-Intensive Workflow Management: For Clouds and Data-Intensive and Scalable Computing Environments
Daniel C.M. de Oliveira, Ji Liu, and Esther Pacitti
2019

Answering Queries Using Views, Second Edition
Foto Afrati and Rada Chirkova
2019

Transaction Processing on Modern Hardware
Mohammad Sadoghi and Spyros Blanas
2019

Data Management in Machine Learning Systems
Matthias Boehm, Arun Kumar, and Jun Yang
2019

Non-Volatile Memory Database Management Systems
Joy Arulraj and Andrew Pavlo
2019

Scalable Processing of Spatial-Keyword Queries
Ahmed R. Mahmood and Walid G. Aref
2019

Data Exploration Using Example-Based Methods
Matteo Lissandrini, Davide Mottin, Themis Palpanas, and Yannis Velegrakis
2018

Data Profiling
Ziawasch Abedjan, Lukasz Golab, Felix Naumann, and Thorsten Papenbrock
2018

Querying Graphs
Angela Bonifati, George Fletcher, Hannes Voigt, and Nikolay Yakovets
2018

Query Processing over Incomplete Databases
Yunjun Gao and Xiaoye Miao
2018

Natural Language Data Management and Interfaces
Yunyao Li and Davood Rafiei
2018

Human Interaction with Graphs: A Visual Querying Perspective
Sourav S. Bhowmick, Byron Choi, and Chengkai Li
2018

On Uncertain Graphs
Arijit Khan, Yuan Ye, and Lei Chen
2018

Answering Queries Using Views
Foto Afrati and Rada Chirkova
2017

Databases on Modern Hardware: How to Stop Underutilization and Love Multicores
Anatasia Ailamaki, Erieta Liarou, Pınar Tözün, Danica Porobic, and Iraklis Psaroudakis
2017

Cloud-Based RDF Data Management

Zoi Kaoudi, Ioana Manolescu, and Stamatis Zampetakis

ISBN: 978-3-031-00747-7   paperback
ISBN: 978-3-031-01875-6   ebook
ISBN: 978-3-031-00102-4   hardcover

DOI 10.1007/978-3-031-01875-6

A Publication in the Springer series
SYNTHESIS LECTURES ON DATA MANAGEMENT

Lecture #62
Series Editor: H.V. Jagadish, *University of Michigan*
Founding Editor: M. Tamer Özsu, *University of Waterloo*
Series ISSN
Print 2153-5418   Electronic 2153-5426

Cloud-Based RDF Data Management

Zoi Kaoudi
Technische Universität Berlin

Ioana Manolescu
INRIA

Stamatis Zampetakis
TIBCO Orchestra Networks

SYNTHESIS LECTURES ON DATA MANAGEMENT #62

ABSTRACT

Resource Description Framework (or RDF, in short) is set to deliver many of the original semi-structured data promises: flexible structure, optional schema, and rich, flexible Universal Resource Identifiers as a basis for information sharing. Moreover, RDF is uniquely positioned to benefit from the efforts of scientific communities studying databases, knowledge representation, and Web technologies. As a consequence, the RDF data model is used in a variety of applications today for integrating knowledge and information: in open Web or government data via the Linked Open Data initiative, in scientific domains such as bioinformatics, and more recently in search engines and personal assistants of enterprises in the form of knowledge graphs.

Managing such large volumes of RDF data is challenging due to the sheer size, heterogeneity, and complexity brought by RDF reasoning. To tackle the size challenge, distributed architectures are required. Cloud computing is an emerging paradigm massively adopted in many applications requiring distributed architectures for the scalability, fault tolerance, and elasticity features it provides. At the same time, interest in massively parallel processing has been renewed by the MapReduce model and many follow-up works, which aim at simplifying the deployment of massively parallel data management tasks in a cloud environment.

In this book, we study the state-of-the-art RDF data management in cloud environments and parallel/distributed architectures that were not necessarily intended for the cloud, but can easily be deployed therein. After providing a comprehensive background on RDF and cloud technologies, we explore four aspects that are vital in an RDF data management system: data storage, query processing, query optimization, and reasoning. We conclude the book with a discussion on open problems and future directions.

KEYWORDS

RDF, cloud computing, MapReduce, key-value stores, query optimization, reasoning

Contents

CHAPTER 1

Introduction

The Resource Description Framework (RDF) [W3C, 2004] first appeared in 2004 to realize the vision of the *Semantic Web* [Berners-Lee et al., 2001]. The goal of Semantic Web was to evolve the Web in order to accommodate intelligent, automatic processes that perform tasks on behalf of the users utilizing *machine-readable data*. This data should have well-defined semantics enabling better data integration and interoperability. RDF provided the standardized means of representing this structured and meaningful information on the Web.

Today a vast amount of data is available online accommodating many aspects of human activities, knowledge, and experiences. RDF provides a simple and abstract knowledge representation for such data on the Web which are uniquely identified by Universal Resource Identifiers (URIs). RDF Schema (RDFS) [W3C, 2014b] is the vocabulary language of RDF. It gives meaning to resources, groups them into concepts and identifies the relationships between these concepts. Web Ontology Language (OWL) [W3C OWL Working Group, 2012] can also be used for conceptualization and provides further expressiveness in stating relationships among the resources. Ontology languages, such as RDFS and OWL, allow for deriving entailed information through *reasoning*. For instance, one can reason that any *student* is also a *human*, or that if X *worksWith* Y, then X also *knows* Y; or that if X *drives* car Z, then X is a *human* and Z is a vehicle. Finally, to be able to explore and query structured information expressed in RDF, SPARQL [W3C, 2013] has been the official W3C recommendation language since 2008.

RDF is used today in a variety of applications. A particularly interesting one comes from the Open Data concept that "*certain data should be freely available to everyone to use and republish as they wish, without restrictions from copyright, patents or other mechanisms of control.*"[1] Open Data federates players of many roles, from organizations such as business and government aiming at demonstrate transparency and good (corporate) governance, to end users interested in consuming and producing data to share with others, to aggregators that may build business models around warehousing, curating, and sharing this data [Raschia et al., 2012]. Sample governmental Open Data portals are the ones from the U.S.,[2] UK,[3] and France.[4] At the same time, if Open Data designates a general philosophy, Linked Data refers to the "*recommended best practice for exposing, sharing, and connecting pieces of data, information, and knowledge on the Semantic Web using URIs and RDF*" [Berners-Lee, 2006]. In practice, Open and Linked data are frequently

---

[1]http://en.wikipedia.org/wiki/Open_data
[2]www.data.gov
[3]www.data.gov.uk
[4]www.etalab.fr

combined to facilitate data sharing, interpretation, and exploitation LOD. Sample applications of Linked Open Data are DBPedia (the Linked Data version of Wikipedia), BBC's platform for the World Cup 2010 and the 2012 Olympic games [Kiryakov et al., 2010].

In addition, RDF is the main data model behind private or public knowledge graphs (e.g., DBPedia [Auer et al., 2007], YAGO [Suchanek et al., 2007], Wikidata[5] (previously Freebase)). Knowledge graphs have been increasingly used recently by enterprises to facilitate and enhance the functionality of their products. Knowledge graphs are simply graphs that connect entities via their relationships. For example, Google uses a knowledge graph in its search engine and personal assistant, Microsoft built a knowledge graph [Gao et al., 2018] used in its products (e.g., Bing and Cortana), and Walmart [Deshpande et al., 2013] and Amazon [Dong, 2018] use knowledge graphs in a variety of applications such as product search and advertising.

To exploit large volumes of RDF data, one could try to build a centralized warehouse. Some of the very first systems that appeared in the Semantic Web community include Jena [Wilkinson et al., 2003] and Sesame [Broekstra and Kampman, 2002]. Later on, RDF-based stores had gained interest in the database community as well, as illustrated by the works of Abadi et al. [2009], Neumann and Weikum [2010b] and Weiss et al. [2008b]. Moreover, commercial database management systems also had started providing support for RDF, such as Oracle 11g [Chong et al., 2005] or IBM DB2 10.1 [Bornea et al., 2013]. These works mostly focused on RDF viewed as a relational database on which to evaluate conjunctive queries and do not consider RDF-specific features such as those related to reasoning. A different line of research focused on viewing RDF as a graph and exploited graph models for the indexing and storage and subgraph matching for querying [Udrea et al., 2007, Zou et al., 2014].

Large and increasing data volumes have also raised the need for distributed storage architectures. Past works on distributed RDF query processing and reasoning have relied on peer-to-peer platforms [Kaoudi and Koubarakis, 2013, Kaoudi et al., 2010] or clustered architectures [Erling and Mikhailov, 2009, Harris et al., 2009, Owens et al., 2008]. Most of these approaches have been proved inadequate to scale to the large amounts of RDF data that we encounter nowadays. Peer-to-peer architectures suffer more on long latency during query evaluation because of the many communication steps required when exchanging large amounts of data and the geo-distribution of peers. Clustered architectures, on the other hand, requires very fine-grained tuning of the cluster and have long loading times.

Cloud computing is an emerging paradigm massively adopted in many applications for the scalability, fault tolerance and elasticity features it offers, which also allows for effortless deployment of distributed and parallel architectures. At the same time, interest in massively parallel processing has been renewed by the MapReduce model [Dean and Ghemawat, 2004] and many follow-up works, which aim at simplifying the deployment of massively parallel data management tasks in a cloud environment. For these reasons, cloud-based stores are an interesting avenue to explore for handling very large volumes of RDF data.

---

[5]https://www.wikidata.org

The main goal of this book is to study *state-of-the-art RDF data management in a cloud environment*. It also investigates the most recent advances of RDF data management in *parallel/distributed architectures* that were not necessarily intended for the cloud, but can easily be deployed therein. We provide a description of existing systems and proposals which can handle large volumes of RDF data while classifying them along different dimensions and highlighting their limitations and opportunities. We start by identifying four dimensions according to the way in which systems implement four fundamental functionalities: *data storage*, *query processing*, *query optimization*, and *reasoning*. Then, within each dimension we classify each system according to their basic characteristics.

The remainder of this book is organized as follows. We start with Chapter 2 by introducing the main features of RDF and its accompanying schema language RDFS. The same chapter gives an overview of the cloud-based frameworks and tools used up through today for RDF data management. In Chapter 3 we present current approaches on RDF data storage and in Chapter 4 we describe different query processing paradigms for evaluating RDF queries. Chapter 5 describes the state-of-the-art in query optimization used for cloud-based query evaluation. In Chapter 6 we lay out the state-of-the-art in RDFS reasoning on top of cloud platforms. Finally, we conclude in Chapter 7 and give insights into open problems and directions.

CHAPTER 2

Preliminaries

This chapter introduces the main concepts of RDF and its accompanying schema language RDFS. It additionally describes the main characteristics of the distributed paradigms and frameworks used in the cloud that have been used in building RDF data management systems.

2.1 RESOURCE DESCRIPTION FRAMEWORK (RDF)

We start by introducing the background for our topic of interest, notably the RDF data model (Section 2.1.1) and SPARQL query language (Section 2.1.2). We then outline the major current architectures for storing and processing data, upon which large-scale RDF data management systems are built (Section 2.2).

2.1.1 DATA MODEL

RDF data is organized in *triples* of the form ($s\ p\ o$), stating that the subject s has the property (a.k.a. predicate) p whose value is the object o. *Unique Resource Identifiers* (URIs) are central in RDF: One can use URIs in any position of a triple to uniquely refer to some entity or concept. Notice that literals (constants) are also allowed in the o position.

RDF allows some form of incomplete information through *blank nodes*, standing for unknown constants or URIs. One may think of blank nodes as *labeled nulls* from the database literature [Abiteboul et al., 1995].

Definition 2.1 RDF Triple. Let U be a set of URIs, L be a set of literals, and B be a set of blank nodes. A well-formed *RDF triple* is a tuple ($s\ p\ o$) from $(U \cup B) \times U \times (U \cup L \cup B)$.

The syntactic conventions for representing valid URIs, literals, and blank nodes can be found in RDF Concepts. In this book, literals are shown as strings enclosed by quotation marks, while URIs are shown as simple strings (see also discussion on namespaces below).

RDF admits a natural graph representation, with each ($s\ p\ o$) triple seen as an p-labeled directed edge from the node identified by s to the node identified by o.

Definition 2.2 RDF Graph. An *RDF graph* is a set of RDF triples.

We use $val(G)$ to refer to the values (URIs, literals, and blank nodes) of an RDF graph G.

```
:sculptor :subClassOf :artist .
:painter :subClassOf :artist .
:cubist :subClassOf :painter.
:paints :subPropertyOf :creates.
:creates :domain :artist.
:creates :range :artifact.
:picasso :type :cubist .
:picasso :name "Pablo" .
:picasso :paints :guernica .
:guernica :type :artifact .
:guernica :exhibited :reinasofia .
:reinasofia :located :madrid .
:rodin :type :sculptor .
:rodin :name "Auguste" .
:rodin :creates :thethinker .
:thethinker :exhibited :museerodin .
:museerodin :located :paris .
```

Figure 2.1: RDF graph in N-Triples syntax.

For instance, Figure 2.1 depicts an RDF graph in the so-called N-Triples syntax, while Figure 2.2 shows a graphical representation of the same graph.

In some cases, we need to work with several RDF graphs while still being able to distinguish the graph each triple originates from. We achieve this by considering *named* RDF graphs where each graph is associated with a name that can be a URI or a blank node. The notion of an RDF triple is extended as follows to capture these needs.

Definition 2.3   RDF quad.   Let U be a set of URIs, L be a set of literals, and B be a set of blank nodes. A well-formed *RDF quad* is a tuple (s p o g) from $(U \cup B) \times U \times (U \cup L \cup B) \times (U \cup B)$.

We are now able to capture multiple RDF graphs using the notion of an RDF dataset.

Definition 2.4   An *RDF dataset* is a set of RDF quads.

An RDF dataset may contain only a single graph, in which case all the quads of the form (s p o g) have the same value for g. In such cases, we may use the term RDF graph and RDF dataset interchangeably.

Namespaces are supported in RDF as a means to support flexible choices of URIs as well as interoperability between different datasets. A namespace typically serves to identify a certain application domain. Concretely, a namespace is identified by a URI, which is used as a prefix of all URIs defined within the respective application domain. Thus, for instance, the URI `http://www.w3.org/1999/02/22-rdf-syntax-ns` is chosen by the W3C to represent the

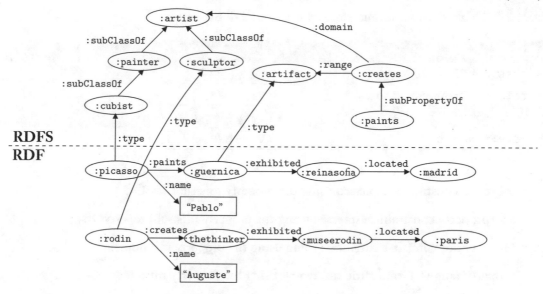

Figure 2.2: Graphical representation of the RDF graph in Figure 2.1.

domain of a small set of predefined URIs which are part of the RDF specification itself; or, for instance, `http://swat.cse.lehigh.edu/onto/univ-bench.owl` is used by the University of Lehigh to identify its domain of representation. To denote that the URI of a resource r is part of the application domain identified by a namespace URI u, the URI of u is a prefix of the URI of r. The suffix of r's URI is typically called *local name*; it uniquely identifies r among all the resources of the namespace u. This enables other application domains to use the same local name in conjunction with their respective namespace URIs without causing confusions between the two. On the other hand, when one wishes to refer in a dataset to a specific resource from a specific namespace, the full URI (including the namespace URI prefix) must be used.

While the above mechanism is flexible, it leads to rather lengthy URIs, which increase the space occupancy of a dataset. To solve this problem, within an RDF graph, a *local namespace prefix* is associated with a namespace URI and serves as a shorthand to represent the latter. Thus, URIs are typically of the form $nsp{:}ln$, where nsp stands for the local namespace prefix while ln represents the local name.

Resource descriptions can be enhanced by specifying to which *class(es)* a given resource belongs by means of the pre-defined rdf:type property which is part of the RDF specification.

For instance, the RDF Graph in Figure 2.1 features the classes `:artist`, `:painter`, `:cubist`, etc., and the resource `:picasso` is stated to be of type `:cubist`.

Further, the RDF Schema [W3C, 2014b] specification allows relating classes and properties used in a graph through ontological (i.e., deductive) constraints expressed as triples using built-in properties:

Table 2.1: Deductive constraints expressible in an RDF Schema

RDFS Constraint	Relational Modeling
`s rdfs:subClassOf o`	$\forall x\ [s(x) \to o(x)]$
`s rdfs:subPropertyOf o`	$\forall x, y\ [s(x, y) \to o(x, y)]$
`p rdfs:domain c`	$\forall x, y\ [p(x, y) \to c(x)]$
`p rdfs:range c`	$\forall x, y\ [p(x, y) \to c(y)]$

- sub-class constraints expressed using the property rdfs:subClassOf;

- sub-property constraints expressed using the property rdfs:subPropertyOf;

- property domain (first attribute) typing using the property rdfs:domain;

- property range (second attribute) typing using the property rdfs:range.

RDFS constraints and their corresponding relational (first-order logic) modeling are given in Table 2.1.

For instance, our sample RDF graph features the subclass constraint `:sculptor rdfs:subClassOf :artist`, and the subproperty constraint `:paints rdfs:subClassOf :creates`. Moreover, it types the first and second attribute of the property `:creates` by stating that someone who creates is an `:artist`, while the creation results in an `:artifact`.

The previous example reveal an important feature of RDF, which is *implicit information*: triples that hold in the RDF graph even though they may not be part of it explicitly. The process of inferring new triples based on existing ones (some of them may be RDF Schema constraints, while the others are simple triples, a.k.a. facts) is known as RDF entailment or *inference* and is guided by a set of entailment rules. Table 2.2 presents the most common RDFS entailment rules. The full set of entailment rules is defined in the RDF Semantics [W3C, 2014a].

The first two rules, s_1 and s_2, start from premises that are schema triples and lead to another schema triple; they can be seen as reasoning on the RDF Schema itself. For instance, if we know that `:cubist rdfs:subClassOf :painter` and `:painter rdfs:subClassOf :artist`, it is easy to see that `:cubist rdfs:subClassOf :artist`.

The remaining rules i_1 to i_4 apply on one data and one schema triple, and lead to a new data triple. Rule i_1 infers that resource s is of type c_2, if s is of a type c_1 that is more specific than c_2. For instance, in our sample graph, if `:picasso rdf:type :cubist` and `:cubist rdfs:subClassOf :painter`, then `:picasso rdf:type :painter`. Rule i_2 states that the property p_2 of a resource s is o as soon as p_1 is a subproperty of p_2 and o is the value of the property p_2 of s. For instance, if `:picasso :paints :guernica`, it is also the case that `:picasso :creates :guernica`. Rule i_3 allows us to infer that a resource s is of type c if s has a property p whose domain is c. For instance, given that `:creates` has the domain `:artist`, and knowing that `:rodin :creates :thethinker`, it

Table 2.2: Entailment rules based on RDFS constraints.

Rule	Premise (existing triples)	Conclusion (entailed triple)
s_1	(c_1 `rdfs:subClassOf` c_2), (c_2 `rdfs:subClassOf` c_3)	(c_1 `rdfs:subClassOf` c_3)
s_2	(p_1 `rdfs:subPropertyOf` p_2), (p_2 `rdfs:subPropertyOf` p_3)	(p_1 `rdfs:subPropertyOf` p_3)
i_1	(c_1 `rdfs:subClassOf` c_2), (s `rdf:type` c_1)	(s `rdf:type` c_2)
i_2	(p_1 `rdfs:subPropertyOf` p_2), (s p_1 o)	(s p_2 o)
i_3	(p `rdfs:domain` c), (s p o)	(s `rdf:type` c)
i_4	(p `rdfs:range` c), (s p o)	(o `rdf:type` c)

follows that `:rodin` is of type `:artist`. Finally, rule i_4 allows us to infer that a resource o is of type c if o is a value of a property p whose range is c. For example, given that `:thethinker` is created by someone, and knowing that the range of `:creates` is `:artifact`, we can infer that `:thethinker` is an `:artifact`.

Note that in this example, there were two independent ways of inferring that `:rodin` `rdf:type` `:artist`, one based on rule i_3 as explained above, and another one based on the rule i_1, knowing that `:rodin` is a `:sculptor` and that every `sculptor` is an `artist`. More generally, although in our example this is not the case, the RDF graph may even have contained the explicit fact `:rodin` `rdf:type` `:artist`. Thus, in an arbitrary RDF graph, the same fact may be present only explicitly, or only implicitly, and there may be several ways to infer the same fact from those explicitly present in the graph.

Observe that unlike the traditional setting of relational databases, RDF Schema constraints are expressed with RDF triples themselves and are part of the RDF graph (as opposed to relational schemas being separated from the relational database instances). Within an RDF dataset, the term *fact* is commonly used to denote a triple whose property is not one of the predefined RDF Schema properties.

Definition 2.5   RDFS Closure.   The RDFS closure of an RDF graph G, denoted G^∞, is obtained by adding to G all the implicit triples that derive from consecutive applications of the entailment rules on G until a fixpoint is reached.

It has been shown that under RDF Schema constraints, the closure of an RDF graph is finite and unique (up to blank node renaming) [Muñoz et al., 2009, ter Horst, 2005b]. For instance, Figure 2.3 depicts the RDFS closure of the RDF graph shown in Figure 2.1. In Figure 2.3, the inferred triples that were not already present in the initial RDF graph are shown in italic font.

```
:sculptor :subClassOf :artist .
:painter :subClassOf :artist .
:cubist :subClassOf :painter.
:cubist :subClassOf :painter .
:paints :subPropertyOf :creates.
:creates :domain :artist.
:creates :range :artifact.
:picasso :type :cubist .
:picasso :type :painter .
:picasso :type :artist .
:picasso :name "Pablo" .
:picasso :paints :guernica .
:picasso :creates :guernica .
:guernica :type :artifact .
:guernica :exhibited :reinasofia .
:reinasofia :located :madrid .
:rodin :type :sculptor .
:rodin :type :artist .
:rodin :name "Auguste" .
:rodin :creates :thethinker .
:thethinker :type :artifact .
:thethinker :exhibited :museerodin .
:museerodin :located :paris .
```

Figure 2.3: **RDFS closure of the RDF graph in Figure 2.1.**

2.1.2   THE SPARQL QUERY LANGUAGE

The advent of the Semantic Web along with the arrival of the RDF data model entailed the need for a suitable declarative query language. SPARQL [W3C, 2008], which became a W3C standard in 2008, has evolved since its proposal; the current version (SPARQL 1.1 [W3C, 2013]) resembles a complex relational query language such as SQL.

SPARQL has a variety of features. The simplest ones are: conjunctive graph pattern matching, selections, projections, and joins, while the more advanced allow arithmetic and alphanumeric comparisons, aggregations, nested sub-queries, and graph construction. In this work, we consider the most common fragment of SPARQL, named *basic graph pattern (BGP)* queries; from a database perspective, these correspond to conjunctive select-project-join (SPJ) queries.

A central role in composing BGPs is played by triple patterns.

Definition 2.6   Triple Pattern.   Let U be a set of URIs, L be a set of literals and V be a set of variables, a *triple pattern* is a tuple $(s\ p\ o)$ from $(U \cup V) \times (U \cup V) \times (U \cup L \cup V)$.

```
SELECT ?a ?c
WHERE { ?c :creates ?a . ?a :exhibited ?m . ?m :locatedIn :paris . }
```

Figure 2.4: Sample RDF query QA.

Triple patterns are used to specify queries against a single RDF graph. Going forward, when no confusion arises, we refer to BPG patterns as triple patterns or even simply atoms/triples.

Based on triple (or quad) patterns, one can express SPARQL BGP queries as below.

Definition 2.7 BGP Query.   A *BGP query* is an expression of the form

$$\text{SELECT } ?x_1,\ldots, ?x_m \text{ WHERE } \{ t_1,\ldots,t_n \}$$

where $t_1,\ldots,t_n$ are triple patterns and $?x_1,\ldots,x_m$ are distinguished variables appearing in $t_1,\ldots,t_n$. We also define the *size of the query* as its number of distinct triple patterns.

Alternatively, for ease of presentation, BGP queries can be represented using the equivalent conjunctive query notation, e.g., the query appearing in Definition 2.7 could be denoted as $q(x_1,\ldots,x_m) \leftarrow t_1 \ldots t_n$.

In the remainder we use the terms *RDF query*, *SPARQL query*, and *BGP query*, interchangeably referring to the SPARQL fragment described by Definition 2.7. Furthermore, we use *varq* (resp. *vart$_i$*) to refer to the variables of a query q (resp. an atom t_i). Additionally, we refer to the set of head variables of q as $headvar(q)$.

An example BGP query, asking for the resources exhibited in Paris and their creators, is shown in Figure 2.4.

Definition 2.8 Valid Assignment.   Let q be a BGP query, and G be an RDF graph, $\mu : var(q) \rightarrow val(G)$ *is a valid assignment* iff $\forall t_i \in q,\ t_i^{\mu} \in G$ where we denote by t_i^{μ} the result of replacing every occurrence of a variable $e \in var(q)$ in the triple pattern t_i by the value $\mu(e) \in val(G)$.

Definition 2.9 Result Tuple.   Let q be a BGP query, G be an RDF graph, μ be a valid assignment, and $\bar{x} = headvarq$, the *result tuple of q based on μ*, denoted as $res(q,\mu)$, is the tuple:

$$res(q,\mu) = \{\mu(x_1),\ldots,\mu(x_m) \mid x_1,\ldots,x_m \in \bar{x}\}$$

Definition 2.10 Query Evaluation.   Let q be a BGP query, and G be an RDF graph, the *evaluation of q against G* is:

$$q(G) = \{res(q,\mu) \mid \mu : var(q) \rightarrow val(G) \text{ is a valid assignment}\}$$

where $res(q, \mu)$ is the result tuple of q based on μ.

The evaluation of query QA (shown in Figure 2.4) against the graph of Figure 2.1 is the tuple `:rodin :thethinker`.

Query evaluation only accounts for triples explicitly present in the graph. If entailed triples are not explicitly in the graph, evaluating the query may miss some results which would have been obtained otherwise. For instance, consider the query:

```
SELECT ?a
WHERE { ?a rdf:type?artifact . }
```

Evaluating the query on the graph in Figure 2.1 returns `:guernica` but not `:thethinker` because the latter is not explicitly of type `:artifact`. Instead, query answering on the RDFS closure of the graph depicted in Figure 2.3 leads to two answers `:guernica` and `:thethinker`.

The following definition allows capturing results due to both the explicit and implicit triples in an RDF graph:

Definition 2.11 Query Answering.   The *answer of a BGP query q over an RDF graph G* is the evaluation of q over G^∞.

It is worth noting that while the relational SPJ queries are most often used with set semantics, SPARQL, just like SQL, has bag (multiset) semantics.

An alternative strategy to RDFS closure for enabling complete query answering w.r.t. implicit information is known as query reformulation. Query reformulation expands the original query into a reformulated one whose answer over the initial graph is complete.

Definition 2.12 Query Reformulation.   Given a query q and an RDF graph G, a query q^{ref} is a reformulation of q w.r.t. the RDFS constraints of G, iff $q(G^\infty) = q^{ref}(G)$.

Different query reformulation algorithms have been proposed in literature. Reformulating into a union of conjunctive queries (UCQ) applies to various fragments of RDF ranging from Description Logics (DL) to Database [Goasdoué et al., 2013], [Urbani et al., 2013], [Kaoudi et al., 2008], [Urbani et al., 2011b], [De Giacomo et al., 2012], [Adjiman et al., 2007], [Goasdoué et al., 2011], [Calvanese et al., 2007], [Gottlob et al., 2011], [König et al., 2015]. Another notable reformulation technique computes semi-conjunctive queries (SCQ) reformulations [Thomazo, 2013] and can be applied to the DL fragment of RDF. Join of unions of conjunctive queries (JUCQ) reformulation, a generalization of both UCQ and SCQ, has been proposed for RDF [Bursztyn et al., 2015b] and its DL fragment [Bursztyn et al., 2015a], and has shown to be able to improve the execution performance of reformulated queries.

For illustration, the UCQ reformulation of the query asking for artifacts is:

```
SELECT ?a WHERE { { ?a rdf:type:artifact . }
                  UNION { ?a rdf:type:painting . }
                  UNION { ?c :created ?a . }
                  UNION { ?c :painted ?a . } }
```

In the UCQ, all expansions of the original term `?a rdf:type:artifact` are evaluated, and a union of their results is returned. For this very simple one-atom query, the UCQ, SCQ and JUCQ reformulations coincide.

It is easy to see that for more complex queries, each atom may have a large expansion, and the possible combinations among these expansions lead to a potentially large reformulation. The interest of SCQs and JUCQs, which are clearly equivalent to the UCQ reformulation, is to propose different orders among the query operators, which oftentimes lead to more efficient evaluation through a standard RDBMS.

2.2 DISTRIBUTED STORAGE AND COMPUTING PARADIGMS

We now outline the main features of distributed storage and computing paradigms including distributed file systems, key-value stores and computation frameworks.

2.2.1 DISTRIBUTED FILE SYSTEMS

Distributed file systems have their roots way back in the 1980s [Sandberg et al., 1985]. However, the topic has seen renewed interest with the emergence of the cloud computing.

In an attempt to cover growing data processing needs, Google introduced the Google File System [Ghemawat et al., 2003] (GFS), a distributed file system which aims to provide performance, scalability, reliability and availability. However, it makes some radical design choices to support more effectively the following scenarios. First, because it is meant to be deployed on very large sets of standard hardware, node failures are considered the rule rather than the exception. Second, it is assumed that typical files are extremely large (in GBs) while the number of files is rather moderate, thus performance-wise, choices are made to support the large ones. Third, updates are typically handled by appending to the file rather than overwriting.

GFS follows a master/slave architecture. Files are split into fixed-size chunks. Each chunk is given a unique 64-bit Id by the master and the slaves store file chunks on local disk as normal files. For reliability, each file chunk is replicated on multiple servers (3 times by default). The master node keeps all required metadata for placement, replication, reading and writing of file chunks.

In the same spirit, and closely following the GFS design principles, other distributed file systems were developed like Apache's Hadoop Distributed File System [Hadoop] (HDFS), and Amazon's S3 [S3]. HDFS became popular due to the open source implementation that Apache provided.

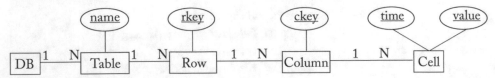

Figure 2.5: ER Diagram for common key-value stores.

Distributed file systems, however, do not provide fine-grained data access, and thus, selective access to a piece of data can only be achieved at the granularity of a file. There have been works like [Dittrich et al., 2010, 2012] which extend Hadoop and improve its data access efficiency with indexing functionality, but the proposed techniques are yet to be adopted by Hadoop's development community.

2.2.2   DISTRIBUTED KEY-VALUE STORES

A key-value store (key-value database) is a system for storing, retrieving, and managing associative arrays. An associative array is a data structure that can hold a set of `{key:value}` pairs such that each possible key appears just once. Other common names for associative arrays include map, dictionary, and symbol table. Key-value stores have been around as long as relational databases. In contrast with relational databases, key-value stores have a very limited application programming interface (API) and the vast majority do not support join operations between different arrays. The most basic operations supported by all key-value stores are `Get(k,v)` and `Put(k,v)`.

Recently, key-value stores gained a lot of popularity due to their simple design, horizontal scaling, and finer control over availability. Google's Bigtable [Chang et al., 2006] inspired many of the key-value stores that are used nowadays. Bigtable takes the idea of associative arrays one step further, defining each array as a sparse, distributed, persistent multidimensional sorted map. The Bigtable's map indexes a value using a triple composed of the row key, column key, and a timestamp. Each map implies a nested structure of the form `{rowkey:{columnkey:{time:value}}}`. By considering the map (array) as part of the nested structure, the complete BigTable's architecture can be described as `{tablename:{rowkey:{columnkey:{time:value}}}}`. Using the ER diagram formalism, key-value stores similar to BigTable adopt the schema shown in Figure 2.5.

Popular key-value stores that have been used by RDF systems include: Apache's Cassandra [Cassandra], Apache's Accumulo [Accumulo], Apache's HBase [HBase], Amazon's SimpleDB [SimpleDB], and Amazon's DynamoDB [Dynamo]. Although they share the basic elements of their interfaces, these systems differ with respect to their internal architecture, access control policies, authentication, consistency, etc. Below we briefly present Accumulo, Cassandra, and HBase, while we provide a slightly more elaborated overview for SimpleDB, and DynamoDB to provide more insight regarding the general API of key-value stores found in the cloud and expose various limitations also present in commercial systems.

HBase is an open-source, distributed, versioned, non-relational database modeled after Google's Bigtable and implemented on top of HDFS. A data row in HBase is composed of a sortable row key and an arbitrary number of columns, which are further grouped into column families. A data cell can hold multiple versions of data which are distinguished by timestamps. Data stored in the same column family are stored together in the file system, while data in different column families might be distributed. HBase provides a B+ tree-like index on the row key by default. HBase supports ACID-level semantics on a per-row basis (row-level consistency). In addition, the notion of coprocessors is introduced, which allow the execution of user code in the context of the HBase processes. The result is roughly comparable to the relational database world's triggers and stored procedures.

Accumulo is very similar to HBase since it also follows the Bigtable design pattern and is implemented on top of HDFS. In contrast with HBase and Bigtable, it also provides a server-side programming mechanism, called iterator, that helps increase performance by performing large computing tasks directly on the servers and not on the client machine. By doing this, it avoids sending large amounts of data across the network. Furthermore, it extends the Bigtable data model, adding a new element to the key called "Column Visibility." This element stores a logical combination of security labels that must be satisfied at query time in order for the key and value to be returned as part of a user request. This allows data with different security requirements to be stored in the same table. As a consequence, users can see only those keys and values for which they are authorized.

Cassandra is also inspired by Bigtable and implemented on top of HDFS, thus sharing a lot of similarities with Accumulo and HBase. Nevertheless, it has some distinctive features. It extends the Bigtable data model by introducing supercolumns. A storage model with supercolumns looks like: `{rowkey:{superkey:{columnkey:value}}}`. Supercolumns can be either stored based on the hash value of the supercolumn key or in sorted order. In addition, supercolumns can be further nested. Cassandra natively supports secondary indices, which can improve data access performance in columns whose values have a high level of repetition. Furthermore, it has configurable consistency. Both read and write consistency can be tuned, not only by level, but in extent. Finally, Cassandra provides an SQL-like language, CQL, for interacting with the store.

SimpleDB is a non relational data store provided by Amazon which focuses on high availability (ensured through replication), flexibility, and scalability. SimpleDB supports a set of APIs to query and store items in the database. A SimpleDB data store is organized in domains. Each domain is a collection of items identified by their name. Each item contains one or more attributes; an attribute has a name and a set of associated values. There is a one-to-one mapping from SimpleDB's data model to the one proposed by Bigtable shown in Figure 2.5. Domains correspond to tables, items to rows, attributes to columns, and values to cells. The main operations of SimpleDB API are the following (the respective delete/update operations are also available).

- `ListDomains()` retrieves all the domains associated with one Amazon Web Services (AWS) account.

- `CreateDomain(D)` and `DeleteDomain(D)` respectively creates a new domain D and deletes an existing one.

- `PutAttributes(D, k, (a,v)+)` inserts or replaces attributes (a,v)+ into an item with name k of a domain D. If the item specified does not exist, SimpleDB will create a new item.

- `BatchPutAttributes` performs up to 25 `PutAttributes` operations in a single API call, which allows for obtaining a better throughput performance.

- `GetAttributes(D, k)` returns the set of attributes associated with item k in domain D.

It is not possible to execute an API operation across different domains as it is not possible to combine results from many tables in Bigtable. Therefore, if required, the aggregation of results from API operations executed over different domains has to be done in the application layer. AWS ensures that operations over different domains run in parallel. Hence, it is beneficial to split the data in several domains in order to obtain maximum performance. As with most non-relational databases, SimpleDB does not follow a strict transactional model based on locks or timestamps. It only provides the simple model of conditional puts. It is possible to update fields on the basis of the values of other fields. It allows for the implementation of elementary transactional models such as some entry level versions of optimistic concurrency control.

AWS imposes some size and cardinality limitations on SimpleDB. These limitations include:

- Number of domains: The default settings of an AWS account allow for at most 250 domains. While it is possible to negotiate more, this has some overhead (one must discuss with a sale representative etc.—it is not as easy as reserving more resources through an online form).

- Domain size: The maximum size of a domain cannot exceed 10 GB and the 109 attributes.

- Item name length: The name of an item should not occupy more than 1024 bytes.

- Number of (attribute, value) pairs in an item: This cannot exceed 256. As a consequence, if an item has only one attribute, that attribute cannot have more than 256 associated values.

- Length of an attribute name or value: This cannot exceed 1024 bytes.

DynamoDB   is the successor of SimpleDB that resulted from combining the best parts of the original Dynamo [DeCandia et al., 2007] design (incremental scalability, predictable high performance) with the best parts of SimpleDB (ease of administration of a cloud service, consistency, and a table-based data model that is richer than a pure key-value store).

The main operations of the DynamoDB API are the following (the respective delete/update operations are also available):

- `ListTables()` retrieves all the tables associated with one AWS account in a specific AWS Region.

- `createTable(T, Key(pk, rk?))` creates a new table `T` having a primary key `pk` and a range key `rk`.

- `PutItem(T, Key(hk, [rk]), (a,v)+)` creates a new item in the table `T` containing a set of attributes `(a,v)+` and having a key composed by a hash key `hk` and range key `rk`, or replaces it if it already existed. Specifying the range key is optional.

- `BatchWriteItem(item+)` puts and/or deletes up to 25 items in a single request, thus obtaining better performance.

- `GetItem(T, Key(hk, [rk]), (a)*)`   returns   the   item   having   the   key   `Key(hk, [rk])` in table `T`. Again, specifying the range key is optional. It is possible to retrieve only a subset of the attributes associated with an item by specifying their names `(a)*` in the request.

DynamoDB was designed to provide seamless scalability and fast, predictable performance. It runs on solid state disks (SSDs) for low-latency response times, and there is no limit on the request capacity or storage size for a given table. This is because Amazon DynamoDB automatically partitions the input data and workload over a sufficient number of servers to meet the provided requirements. In contrast with its predecessor (SimpleDB), DynamoDB does not automatically build indexes on item attributes leading to more efficient insert, delete, and update operations, as well as improving the scalability of the system. Indexes can still be created if requested.

2.2.3   DISTRIBUTED COMPUTATION FRAMEWORKS: MAPREDUCE AND BEYOND

MapReduce   MapReduce is probably the best-known framework for massively parallel computation. Its roots in some sense can be traced back to the LISP [McCarthy, 1960] functional programming language; core concepts in functional programming are *map* (to distribute the computation of a function over a list of inputs) and *reduce* (to aggregate such function results). Inspired by the simplicity of this model, Google proposed the MapReduce framework [Dean and Ghemawat, 2004] for processing and generating large data sets. MapReduce resulted from a need to easily parallelize tasks in a large cluster of commodity computers without deep knowledge of parallel and distributed systems. Users write MapReduce programs using the map and reduce primitive operations, and the framework is responsible for parallelizing the program, saving the user from tasks like resource allocation, synchronization, fault tolerance, etc.

A MapReduce program is defined by *jobs*, each of which consists of three main phases:

- A *map* phase, where the input is divided into sub-inputs, each handled by a different map task. The map task takes as input key/value pairs, processes them (by applying the operations defined by the user), and again outputs key/value pairs.

- A *shuffle* phase, where the key/value pairs emitted by the mappers are grouped and sorted by key, and are then assigned to reducers.

- A *reduce* phase, where each reduce task receives key/value pairs (sharing the same key) and applies further user-defined operations, writing the results into the file system.

To store inputs and outputs of MapReduce tasks, a distributed file system (e.g., GFS, HDFS, S3) is typically used.

Many recent massively parallel data management systems leverage MapReduce in order to build scalable query processors for both relational [Li et al., 2014] and RDF [Kaoudi and Manolescu, 2015] data. The most popular open-source implementation of MapReduce is provided by the Apache's Hadoop [Hadoop] framework, used by many RDF data management platforms [Goasdoué et al., 2015, Huang et al., 2011, Husain et al., 2011, Kim et al., 2011, Lee and Liu, 2013, Papailiou et al., 2012, 2013, 2014, Ravindra et al., 2011, Rohloff and Schantz, 2010, Schätzle et al., 2011, Wu et al., 2015].

Following the success of MapReduce proposal, other systems and models have emerged, which extend its expressive power and eliminate some of its shortcomings. Among the most well-known frameworks are the Apache projects Flink (previously known as Stratosphere) [Alexandrov et al., 2014] and Spark [Zaharia et al., 2010].

Spark   Spark achieves orders of magnitude better performance than Hadoop thanks to its main-memory resilient distributed dataset (RDD) [Zaharia et al., 2012]. RDDs are parallel data structures that lets users persist intermediate results in memory and manipulate them using a rich set of operators. They provide fault tolerance via keeping lineage information. Spark's programming model extends the MapReduce model by also including traditional relational operators (e.g., groupby, filter, join). Operations are either *transformations* or *actions*. Transformations (e.g., map, reduce, join) are performed in a lazy execution mode, i.e., they are not executed until an action operator (e.g., collect, count) is called. Spark has gained a lot of popularity for supporting interactive ad hoc batch analytics.

Flink   At the core of the Flink platform lies the PACT (*Pa*rallelization Contra*ct*s) parallel computing model [Battré et al., 2010], which can be seen as a generalization of MapReduce.

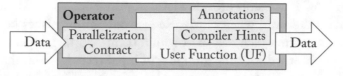

Figure 2.6: PACT operator outline.

PACT plans are built of *implicitly parallel data processing operators* that are optimized and translated into *explicitly parallel data flows* by the Flink platform. PACT operators manipulate *record*s made of several fields; each field can be either an atomic value or a list of records. Optionally, the records in a given record multiset[1] may have an associated *key*, consisting of a subset of the atomic fields in those records.

The data input to/output by a PACT operator is stored in a (distributed) file. A *PACT plan* is a directed acyclic graph (DAG, in short) of operators, where each operator may have one or multiple inputs; this contrast with the "linear" pattern of MapReduce programs, where a single Reduce consumes the output of each Map. As Figure 2.6 shows, a PACT consists of a *parallelization contract*, a *user function* (UF in short), and possibly some *annotations* and *compiler hints* characterizing the UF behavior. The PACT parallelization contract describes how input records are organized into *groups* (prior to the actual processing performed by the operator). A simple possibility is to group the input records by the value(s) of some attribute(s), as customary in MapReduce, but in PACT other choices are also possible. The user function is executed independently over groups of records created by the parallelization contract; therefore these executions can take place in parallel. Finally, annotations and/or compiler hints may be used to enable optimizations (with no impact on the semantics), thus we do not discuss them further.

Although the PACT model allows creating custom parallelization contracts, a set of them for the most common cases is built in:

- The *Map* contract has a single input and builds a singleton for each input record.

- The *Reduce* contract also has a single input; it groups together all records that share the same key.

- The *Cross* contract builds the cartesian product of two inputs, that is: for each pair of records, one from each input, it produces a group containing these two records.

- The *Match* contract builds all pairs of records from its two inputs, having the same key value.

- The *CoGroup* contract can be seen as a "Reduce on two inputs;" it groups the records from both inputs, sharing the same key value.

[1]Similarly to SQL and SPARL but differently from the classical relational algebra, PACT operates on bags (multisets) of records rather than sets.

Observe that PACT operators provide a level of abstraction above MapReduce by manipulating fine-granularity records, whereas MapReduce only distinguishes keys and values (but does not model the structure which may exist within them). Further, separating the input contract (which is only concerned with the grouping of input records) from the actual processing applied in parallel by the operators enables on one hand flexible adaptation to parallel processing, and on the other hand, smooth integration of user functions; this gives significant generality to the PACT model.

2.3   SUMMARY

We have presented all the necessary preliminaries for RDF and the cloud. Given these foundations, the reader should be able to follow the next chapters.

In summary, RDF data is organized in *triples* of the form (s p o), stating that the subject s has the property (a.k.a. predicate) p whose value is the object o. RDF data can also be seen as graphs with s and o being nodes connected with a directed edge from s to o labeled with p. RDF Schema defines classes as groups of entities and properties as relations among classes. Its deductive rules lead to new information being inferred through a reasoning process. SPARQL is a declarative query language for exploring and querying RDF data which mainly consists of a set of triple patterns, i.e., triples which can contain variables.

To set the background for processing in the cloud we have introduced: (i) existing distributed file systems, such as HDFS and S3, (ii) the concept of distributed key-value stores and some stores commonly found in the cloud, such as HBase and DynamoDB, and (iii) distributed computation frameworks, such as MapReduce and Spark. All these components are used by the state-of-the-art distributed RDF data management systems that we will detail in the following.

CHAPTER 3

Cloud-Based RDF Storage

This chapter focuses on the storage components of the existing RDF cloud data management systems. The storage component has an important impact on the performance of data access, and thus on query evaluation performance. We classify existing systems along two orthogonal dimensions:

1. Each system stores a given RDF graph data in one or more fragments (or partitions). According to the way in which the set of triples of each partition is defined, we distinguish:

   • logical partitioning: each set can be described by a first-order logic query over the graph triples and

   • graph-based partitioning: sets are built by inspecting the connections among the graph nodes.

2. Each RDF cloud platform relies on a concrete system for storing its RDF partitions; the functionalities of the latter may be very advanced or on the contrary quite basic. The following alternatives have been investigated for the purpose of storing the data:

   • a distributed file system,

   • a key-value store,

   • a set of distributed RDF databases, typically one on each node participating to the cloud RDF store, and

   • hybrid choices which include one or several distributed systems as above, and in some cases complement it with a single centralized system.

Figure 3.1 illustrates a taxonomy of the storage alternatives and the partitioning schemes currently used in each one. Section 3.1 describes the two partitioning strategies, while Sections 3.2–3.6 describe the storage alternatives used for storing the data.

3.1 PARTITIONING STRATEGIES

In this section, before describing the logical and graph-based partitioning methods, we first present a grammar for concisely describing different partitioning methods and storage structures.

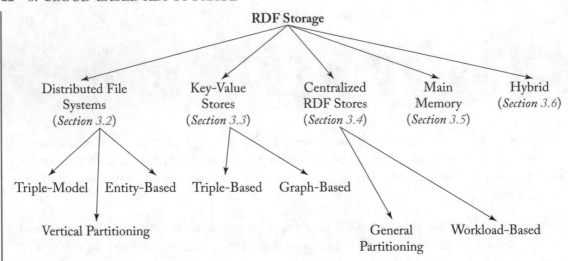

Figure 3.1: Taxonomy of storage schemes.

3.1.1   STORAGE DESCRIPTION GRAMMAR

We have devised a grammar (Definition 3.1) which allows us to describe storage structures produced by any partitioning method.

Definition 3.1   Storage description grammar.   We describe data partitioning methods based on a context-free grammar consisting of the following rules (where X denotes a terminal and <X> is a non-terminal symbol):

$$
\begin{aligned}
&\text{<DSC>} &\rightarrow\quad &\text{<EXP> (\{<EXP>\})?}\\
&\text{<EXP>} &\rightarrow\quad &\text{(<NAM>)? <ATT>+ | (<NAM>)? <M>(<ATT>+)}\\
&\text{<M>} &\rightarrow\quad &\text{HP | CP | GP}\\
&\text{<ATT>} &\rightarrow\quad &\text{S | P | O | U | T | C | G | }\vec{S}\text{ | }\vec{P}\text{ | }\vec{O}\text{ | }\vec{U}\text{ | }\vec{T}\text{ | }\vec{C}\text{ | }\vec{G}\text{ | *}\\
&\text{<NAM>} &\rightarrow\quad &\text{[A-Z]+ | }\epsilon
\end{aligned}
$$

We present the grammar elements in bottom-up fashion, starting from the simplest elements and gradually increasing complexity. Among the terminal symbols of the grammar, we use S to denote the subject values, P for the property values, O for the object values, U for resource (any URI appearing as subject, property, or object in a graph), T for term (any URIs or literal appearing anywhere in the graph), C to denote a class appearing in the graph, and G to refer to the name (or ID) of the graph itself. Further, curly brackets {, } and parentheses (,) are also terminal symbols of the grammar.

The core non-terminal symbol is <ATT>, which specifies an attribute stored within a given storage structure. Its value ranges over the terminals S, P, O, U, T, C, G, to which we add a set of corresponding symbols $\vec{S}$, $\vec{P}$, $\vec{O}$ | $\vec{U}$, $\vec{T}$ | $\vec{C}$, and $\vec{G}$: Each of these denotes that data is stored *sorted* according to the value of the respective information item (S, P etc.) Further, <ATT> may be simply specified using the asterisk (*) symbol to denote that the complete content of a (sub-)graph is stored (instead of writing SPO or SPOG). We use * only when the order in which data is stored is not important.

The non-terminal symbol <EXP> comprises:

- optionally, a storage structure name (<NAM>);

- optionally, a partitioning method specification (<M>), in which case we use parentheses to determine the scope of the partitioning (described below); and

- one or several attribute specifications (<ATT>) as above.

The <M> symbol is used to describe the method used to distribute triples across the distributed store. Two types of methods have been used:

- Hash Partitioning (denoted HP), where the stored tuples are split in partitions based on the value of a hash function on some of their attributes;

- Capacity Partitioning (denoted CP), where partitions are formed solely with the goal of fitting a given capacity on each site, without a specific policy on what data goes in each partition; and

- Graph Partitioning (denoted GP), where partitions are formed based on the connections among the graph nodes.

Sample productions matching the <EXP> non-terminal include: (i) SO or OS denote an anonymous (unnamed) storage structure that stores (subject, object) pairs, (ii) Triples{SPO} represents a data structure named T̲r̲i̲p̲l̲e̲s̲ holding all triples of the dataset, (iii) $\vec{S}$O and O$\vec{S}$ both denote an anonymous storage structure comprising (subject, object) pairs, sorted in the order determined by the subject, (iv) HP(SO) denotes a data structure storing the subject and object of all triples from the graph, partitioned by the subject and object; there are as many fragments in this data structure as there are distinct (subject, object) value combinations.

Note that in a combination of ATT symbols where several have overhead arrows, *the order of such symbols in the combination denotes the order according to which data is sorted in the respective storage structure.* For example, $\vec{O}\,\vec{S}$ denotes (subject, object) pairs sorted first by the object and then by the subject, whereas $\vec{S}\,\vec{O}$ denotes a set of such pairs sorted first by the subject and then by the object. Equivalently, we may also write $\overrightarrow{OS}$ to denote the former or $\overrightarrow{SO}$, to denote the latter.

Finally, <DSC> is a storage structure description. In its simple case, the storage structure is a collection of items, in which case a single <EXP> is sufficient to describe it; or a map, in which case it is specified by two <EXP> symbols, one for the key and one for the value of the map. Note that the second <EXP> may in turn be either a collection or a map, thus allowing for nested maps, or a map where a value is a collection of maps, etc.

3.1.2   LOGICAL PARTITIONING

Popular methods of partitioning an RDF graph into fragments are based on the subject, property, and object values of the RDF triples; when storing several RDF graphs, the graph ID is also included in the store. Grouping is oftentimes used to gain space. For instance, instead of storing all the triples whose subject is :rodin (which leads to repeatedly storing the URI for :rodin), it is more space-efficient to store :rodin only once together with all its properties, and with all the values of these properties. When the partition data is stored in a certain order, that order is usually exploited by the query processor to allow the usage of efficient processing methods such as order-based joins.

The simplest meaningful storage description expression is SPO, which denotes a data structure storing all the (full) triples, with no partitioning. We use S{PO} and P{SO} to describe a system which stores triples twice: first, properties and objects grouped by the subject; second, subjects and objects grouped by their properties. S{P{O}} specifies that triples are first grouped by subject; then, within each group, we split the triples again by the values of their properties, and for each such property we store the set of object values. The resulting data organization can be seen as a multiple-level map, or a two-level index. More examples will be provided when discussing partitioning choices made by concrete storage subsystems.

3.1.3   GRAPH PARTITIONING

Graph partitioning comprises a wide set of algorithms which given a graph, proposes a decomposition thereof in several smaller graphs, aiming to optimize objectives such as: number of edges connecting nodes from different groups of the partition; subgraphs of about the same size; strength of the connections between nodes in the same subgraph, etc. Graph partitioning is in general non-deterministic polynomial (NP-hard), thus the focus is on finding efficient heuristics; many have been proposed and implemented recently, especially given the interest in analyzing and clustering social or communication networks.

One of the first and best-known graph partitioning techniques is METIS[1] [Karypis and Kumar, 1998], which aims at partitions of a bounded size and reducing edges across subgraphs, and which has been used in several platforms we discuss below. One limitation of METIS and other similar methods is that the graph to be partitioned must fit in the memory available to the partitioning algorithm. To overcome this limitation there are streaming partitioning approaches that have been proposed in the literature such as Stanton and Kliot [2012], Tsourakakis et al. [2014].

---

[1]http://glaros.dtc.umn.edu/gkhome/project/gp/overview

3.2   STORING IN DISTRIBUTED FILE SYSTEMS

As discussed in Section 2.2.1, distributed file systems (DFS) are designed for providing scalable and reliable data access in a cluster of commodity machines and, thus, they are a good fit for storing large files of RDF data in the cloud. Large files are split into smaller chunks of data, distributed among the cluster machines and automatically replicated by the DFS for fault-tolerance reasons. As distributed file systems do not provide fine-grained data access, and thus, selective access to a piece of data can only be achieved at the granularity of a file, the RDF community has recently paid more attention to distributed key-value stores for selective data access.

Still, there are systems that use DFS to store RDF data due to its ease of use. We classify these systems according to the way they model the data as follows: (i) the triple model, which preserves the triple construct of RDF, (ii) the vertical partitioning model, which splits RDF triples based on their property, and (iii) the entity-based model, which uses a high-level entity graph to partition the RDF triples.

3.2.1   TRIPLE MODEL

The simplest way to store RDF data into a DFS is to serialize it in a file containing the descriptions of all the triples and uploading that file into the DFS. The file system is then in charge of splitting the files into blocks of similar sizes, replicating them and placing them at the cluster nodes. Conceptually, this can be compared to storing all triples in a plain three-attribute relational table in a centralized setting, but using a distributed (as opposed to a centralized) file system. Such distributed file system stores can be described using our grammar as: CP(SPO), or CP(*).

Systems based on this kind of storage scheme include Rohloff and Schantz [2010], Schätzle et al. [2011], which use the Hadoop Distributed File System (HDFS). In SHARD [Rohloff and Schantz, 2010] a slight variation is used where triples having the same subject are grouped in one line in the file. For instance, for the subject :picasso in our running example of Figure 2.2, SHARD would store the following in one line in an HDFS file:

```
:picasso :paints :guernica :name ``Pablo" :type :cubist.
```

In terms of our grammar, the SHARD variation above corresponds to: CP(S){PO}.

3.2.2   VERTICAL PARTITIONING MODEL

A more elaborate way to store RDF data into a DFS is to partition it into smaller files and thus, enable finer granularity access to the data. To achieve this, RDF triples are partitioned based on their property, and each partition is stored within one file into the DFS, named according to the respective property value. As the predicate can explicitly be inferred from the file name, the predicate-partitioned files need only to store the subject and object of each triple, a factorization which reduces the size of the stored data. For example, for the triples of Figure 2.1, the file "exhibited" contains the following lines:

```
:guernica :reinasofia .
:thethinker :museerodin .
```

The above vertical partitioning scheme is used by systems described in Husain et al. [2011], Ravindra et al. [2011], Zhang et al. [2012]. It is also reminiscent of the vertical RDF partitioning proposed in Abadi et al. [2007], Theoharis et al. [2005] for centralized RDF stores. Such a storage can be described as HP(P){SO} if one considers (as is usually the case) that the value of the property is used for a hash-based assignment of files to the cluster nodes.

Following the predicate-based partitioning scheme, all triples using the built-in special RDF predicate :type are located in the same partition. However, because such triples appear very frequently in RDF datasets, this leads to a single very big file containing such triples. In addition, most triple patterns in SPARQL queries having :type as a predicate usually have the object bound as well. This means that a search for atoms of the form (:x, :type, :t1), where :t1 is a concrete URI, in the partition corresponding to the :type predicate is likely to be inefficient. For this reason, in HadoopRDF [Husain et al., 2011] the :type partition is further split based on the object value of the triples. For example, the triple (:picasso, :type, :cubist) is stored in a file named "type#cubist" which holds all the instances of class :cubist. This partitioning is performance-wise interesting for the predicate :type because the object of such triples is an RDFS class and the number of distinct classes appearing in the object position of :type triples is typically moderate. Clearly, such a partitioning is less interesting for properties having a large number of distinct object values, as this would lead to many small files in the DFS. In general, having many small files in the DFS leads to a significant overhead at the server (the so-called *namenode*), and thus should be avoided.

HadoopRDF [Husain et al., 2011] goes one step further by splitting triples that have the same predicate based also on the RDFS class the object belongs to (if such information exists). This can be determined by inspecting all the triples having predicate :type. For example, the triple (:picasso, :paints, :guernica) would be stored in a file named "paints#artifact" because of the triple (:guernica, :type, :artifact). This grouping helps for query minimization purposes, as we shall see in Section 4.1.1.

Predicate-based partitioning is clearly helpful in order to provide selective data access; however, in distributed systems this partitioning cannot help with data locality issues. Triples with the same predicate are guaranteed to be at the same node, but SPARQL queries typically involve more than one predicate. Such queries will have to shuffle large amounts of data in order to evaluate the query. CliqueSquare [Goasdoué et al., 2015], inspired by works like Cai and Frank [2004] which store RDF in P2P networks, minimizes network traffic by extending the predicate-based partitioning of HadoopRDF with an additional hash-partitioning scheme as follows.

First, CliqueSquare replicates the data three times, and each copy is partitioned in a different way: by the subject, the property, and the object, respectively. Each copy of the data is distributed among the available machines by hashing their partitions, based on the values of

Table 3.1: Hash partitioning of RDF triples in 3 nodes

Node 1	Node 2	Node 3
:sculptor :subClassOf :artist	:sculptor :subClassOf :artist	:sculptor :subClassOf :artist
:painter :subClassOf :artist	:painter :subClassOf :artist	:painter :subClassOf :artist
:cubist :subClassOf :painter	:cubist :subClassOf :painter	
:cubist :subClassOf :painter		
:paints :subPropertyOf :creates.	:paints :subPropertyOf :creates.	:paints :subPropertyOf :creates
	:creates :domain :artist	:creates :domain :artist
		:creates :domain :artist
:creates :range :artifact	:creates :range :artifact	:creates :range :artifact
:picasso :type :cubist	:picasso :type :cubist	
:picasso :type :cubist		
:picasso :name "Pablo"	:picasso :name "Pablo"	:picasso :name "Pablo"
:picasso :paints :guernica		
:picasso :paints :guernica	:picasso :paints :guernica	
:guernica :type :artifact	:guernica :type :artifact	
	:guernica :type :artifact	
:guernica :exhibited :reinasofia	:guernica :exhibited :reinasofia	:guernica :exhibited :reinasofia
:reinasofia :located :madrid	:reinasofia :located :madrid	:reinasofia :located :madrid
:rodin :type :sculptor	:rodin :type :sculptor	:rodin :type :sculptor
:rodin :name "Auguste"	:rodin :name "Auguste"	:rodin :name "Auguste"
	:rodin :creates :thethinker	:rodin :creates :thethinker
		:rodin :creates :thethinker
:thethinker :exhibited :museerodin	:thethinker :exhibited :museerodin	:thethinker :exhibited :museerodin
:museerodin :located :paris	:museerodin :located :paris	:museerodin :located :paris

the subject, property, and object, respectively. Table 3.1 shows the triples of the running example partitioned across three machines; the partition attribute appears underlined. Observe that triples having the same value in the subject, property, or object position are guaranteed to be at the same node.

Second, at each node, a separate file will be created for each predicate present on that node, in a fashion reminiscent to that of HadoopRDF. For instance, continuing with our example, node 1 will have a file named "1_name-S" holding triple :picasso :name ``Pablo", and a file named "1_name-O" holding the triple :rodin :name ``Auguste", instead of having a single file "1_name" containing both triples. The extra splitting based on RDFS classses (used in HadoopRDF) is also present in CliqueSquare. In Chapter 5 we shall explain how this additional partitioning step can be exploited by the query optimizer to minimize data shuffling.

An alternative vertical partitioning model would be to partition triples based on their subject or object value, instead of the property. However, this would lead to a high number of very small files because of the number of distinct subject or object values appearing in RDF datasets, which is to be avoided, as explained above. In addition, most SPARQL queries specify the predicate in the triple patterns, while unspecified subject or object values are more common.

Thus, predicate-based partitioning makes selective data access (i.e., access to triples stored in a specific relatively small file) more likely.

An extended version of the vertical partitioning model is proposed in S2RDF [Schätzle et al., 2016], which is built on top of Spark. The basic idea is to precompute semi-join reductions for each type of join (SS, OS, and SO) of all pairs of predicates. These smaller tables determine the contents of a predicate file that are guaranteed to join with the contents of another predicate file. For instance, using our running example (Figure 2.2), S2RDF creates a file "creates-name_SS" which contains the pair :rodin :thinker, which is the result of semi-joining creates with name on the subjects. This reduces the size of input data for a query that needs to join the predicates creates and name on the subjects. To reduce the storage overhead that naturally comes with this scheme, S2RDF supports an optional selectivity threshold which determines when the reduction of the predicate files pays off for the extended files to be materialized.

3.2.3   PARTITIONING BASED ON RDF ENTITIES

Graph partitioning has been combined with *grouping triples in entities* in the EAGRE [Zhang et al., 2013] (Entity-Aware Graph compREssion) system. The authors define an entity as any RDF node together with its (non-empty) set of outgoing properties; thus, an entity is either a resource or a blank node with outgoing properties. This corresponds in term of our partition dialect to S{PO}.

To partition the graph, the authors first categorize the entities in a set of *entity classes*, based on the similarity of their sets of outgoing properties; entities in a single class tend to have a large share of common properties. This is performed by distributing the triples at random in the cluster, then running a MapReduce job computing a similarity join among the nodes. The entity classes lead to a *compressed entity graph*, where each class has a node, and an edge labeled p goes from c_1 to c_2 if and only if for some nodes $n_1 \in c_1$, $n_2 \in c_2$, the original graph includes a triple (:n_1, :p, :n_2). Finally, the compressed entity graph is partitioned using METIS to determine on which machine each entity will reside.

At each node in the distributed system, the storage is designed with two purposes: (i) given a query, efficiently find the data blocks containing triples that match the query (selective data access) and (ii) facilitate answering queries with result order constraints by storing triples in the increasing order of their predicate or object values. To attain these goals, entities in a class, having similar properties, are viewed as high-dimensional data records, and their layout in the file stored at a given node is computed by adapting a specialized multidimensional indexing technique [Lawder and King, 2000], based on the so-called *space filling curves*. Using this layout, access to triples having certain properties with certain values translates to looking up the data at the multidimensional location corresponding to these values, which can be very efficient. The technique may need overflow blocks in case the storage space originally allotted for a spot in the multidimensional space is full and new data is inserted with the same values; a periodic reorganization is proposed by the author.

3.3   STORING IN KEY-VALUE STORES

Key-value stores provide efficient, fine-grained storage and retrieval of data, which fits well with the small granularity of RDF datasets. Key-value stores are thus very good candidates for both storing and indexing RDF data. We classify existing works into *triple-based* and *graph-based* ones: the former treat RDF data as a collection of triples, while the latter adopt a holistic view over the RDF graph.

3.3.1   TRIPLE-BASED

RDF indexing has been thoroughly studied in a centralized setting [Neumann and Weikum, 2010a, Weiss et al., 2008a]. Given the nature of RDF triples, many common RDF indexes store all the RDF dataset itself, eliminating the need for a "store" distinct from the index. Thus, *indexing* RDF in a key-value store is mostly the same as *storing* it there.

As we have seen previously (in Section 2.2.2), key-value stores typically offer four levels of information for structuring the data, i.e., {tablename:{itemkey:{attributename:{attributevalue}}}}. This structure can be easily captured by the storage description grammar from Definition 3.1 as a four-level map. In the following, we use this grammar to present the data layout of the various key-value based systems.

Centralized systems use extensive indexing schemes using all possible permutations of the subject, predicate, object of RDF triples to build indices. For example, Hexastore [Weiss et al., 2008a] uses all $3! = 6$ permutations of subject, predicate, object to build indices that provide fast data access for all possible triple patterns and for efficiently performing merge-joins. RDF-3X [Neumann and Weikum, 2010a] additionally uses aggregated indices on subsets of the subject, predicate, object, resulting in a total of 15 indices. The same indexing scheme has recently migrated to the cloud with H_2RDF+ [Papailiou et al., 2013]. However, this extensive indexing scheme has a significant storage overhead, which is amplified in a distributed environment (where data is replicated for fault tolerance). As a consequence, the majority of existing systems (including the predecessor of H_2RDF+, H_2RDF [Papailiou et al., 2012]) use a more conservative approach with only three indices. The three permutations massively used by today's systems are: subject-predicate-object (SPO), predicate-object-subject (POS), and object-subject-property (OSP). Typical key-value RDF stores materialize each of these permutations in a separate table (collection).

Depending on the specific capabilities of the underlying key-value store, different choices have been made for the keys and values. For example, each one of S, P, O can be used as the key, attribute name, attribute value of the key-value store, or a concatenation of two or even three of the elements can be used as the key. One of the criteria to decide on the design is whether the key-value store offers a hash-based or sorted index. In the first case, only exact lookups are possible and thus, each of the triples' element should be used as the key. In the latter case, combinations of the triples' element can be used since prefix lookup queries can be answered.

Table 3.2: SPO index in a key-value store with a hash index (left) and a sorted index (right)

Item Key	(attr. name, attr. value)	Item Key	(attr. name, attr. value)
:picasso	(:paints, :guernica),	:picasso||:paints||:guernica	(-, -)
	(:name, "Pablo"),	:picasso||:name||"Pablo"	(-, -)
	(:type, :cubist)	:picasso||:type||:cubist	(-, -)
:rodin	(:creates, :thethinker),	:rodin||:creates||:thethinker)	(-, -)
	(:name, "Auguste"),	:rodin||:name||"Auguste"	(-, -)
	(:type, :sculptor)	:rodin||:type||:sculptor	(-, -)
:guernica	(:exhibited, :reinasofia),	:guernica||:exhibited||:reinasofia	(-, -)
	(:type, :artifact)	:guernica||:type||:artifact	(-, -)
:thethinker	(:exhibited, :museerodin)	:thethinker||:exhibited||:museerodin)	(-, -)
:reinasofia	(:located, :madrid)	:reinasofia||:located||:madrid	(-, -)
:museerodin	(:located, :paris)	:museerodin||:located||:paris	(-, -)
:Cubist	(:sc, :painter)	:cubist||:sc||:painter	(-, -)
:Sculptor	(:sc, :artist)	:sculptor||:sc||:artist	(-, -)
:Painter	(:sc, :artist)	:painter||:sc||:artist	(-, -)

The left part of Table 3.2 shows a possible design for the SPO index in a hash-based key-value store using the RDF running example of Figure 2.2. Subjects are used as the keys, predicates are used as the attribute names, and objects as the attribute values. Using our storage description grammar, this index is described as follows: SPO{S{P{O}}}. Similar POS and OSP indices are constructed. When the key-value store offers a sorted index on the key, any concatenation of the triples' elements can be used as the key. In the right part of Table 3.2, we show for the SPO index the extreme case where the concatenation of all three triples' elements are used as the key, while the attribute names and values are empty. The storage descriptor for this index is $\overrightarrow{SPO}$.

Representative systems using key-value stores as their underlying RDF storage facility include Rya [Punnoose et al., 2012], which uses Apache Accumulo [Accumulo]; Cumulus-RDF [Ladwig and Harth, 2011] based on Apache Cassandra [Cassandra]; Stratustore [Stein and Zacharias, 2010b], relying on Amazon's SimpleDB [Amazon Web Services]; H$_2$RDF [Papailiou et al., 2012]; H$_2$RDF+ [Papailiou et al., 2013], built on top of HBase HBase; and AMADA [Aranda-Andújar et al., 2012] which uses Amazon's DynamoDB [Dynamo].

Table 3.3 outlines for each system the key-value store used, the type of index data structure provided by the key-value store, and the storage description. Observe that in some cases some data positions (attribute names and/or attribute values) within the key-value stores are left empty.

Table 3.3: Indices used by RDF systems based on key-value stores

System	Store	Index Type	Storage Description
Rya [Punnoose et al., 2012]	Accumulo [Accumulo]	Sorted	$\overrightarrow{SPO}$, $\overrightarrow{POS}$, $\overrightarrow{OSP}$
H$_2$RDF+ [Papailiou et al., 2012]	HBase [HBase]	Sorted	$\overrightarrow{SP}\{O\}$, $\overrightarrow{PO}\{S\}$, $\overrightarrow{OS}\{P\}$
H$_2$RDF [Papailiou et al., 2013]	HBase [HBase]	Sorted	$\overrightarrow{SPO}$, $\overrightarrow{POS}$, $\overrightarrow{OSP}$ $\overrightarrow{SOP}$, $\overrightarrow{PSO}$, $\overrightarrow{OPS}$
AMADA [Aranda-Andújar et al., 2012]	DynamoDB [Amazon Web Services]	Hash	S{P{O}}, P{O{S}}, O{S{P}}
MAPSIN [Przyjaciel-Zablocki et al., 2012]	HBase [HBase]	Sorted	$\overrightarrow{S}\{P\{O\}\}$, $\overrightarrow{O}\{S\{P\}\}$
Stratustore [Stein and Zacharias, 2010b]	SimpleDB [Amazon Web Services]	Hash	S{P{O}}
CumulusRDF-hierarchical [Ladwig and Harth, 2011]	Cassandra [Cassandra]	Hash/Sorted	S{P{O}}, P{O{S}}, O{S{P}}
CumulusRDF-flat [Ladwig and Harth, 2011]	Cassandra [Cassandra]	Hash/Sorted	S{PO}, PO{S}, O{SP} PO{P{P}}. P{PO}

An important issue in such approaches is the high skewness of the property values, i.e., some property values appear very frequently in the RDF datasets. In this case, a storage scheme using the property as the key leads to a table with few, but very large, rows. Because in HBase all the data of a row is stored at the same machine, machines corresponding to very popular property values may run out of disk space and further cause bottlenecks when processing queries. For this reason, MAPSIN completely discards the POS index, although techniques for handling such skew, e.g., splitting the long list to another machine [Abiteboul et al., 2008], are quite well understood by now. To handle property skew CumulusRDF, built on Cassandra, builds a different POS index. The POS index key is made of the property and object, while the subject is used for the attribute name. Further, another attribute, named P, holds the property value. The secondary index provided by Cassandra, which maps values to keys, is used to retrieve the associated property-object entries for a given property value. This solution prevents overly large property-driven entries, all the while preserving selective access for a given property value. Notice that H$_2$RDF, and H$_2$RDF+, avoid the skew problem by using only the key of HBase;

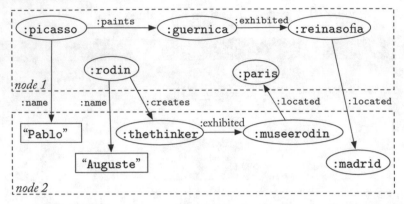

Figure 3.2: RDF graph partitioning in a two-machines cluster of Trinity.RDF.

although they partially lose the locality of some triples, they benefit from a better distribution of rows among machines.

3.3.2   GRAPH-BASED

Graph-oriented storage for RDF data is less studied by the research community but is gaining more attention lately. Unsurprisingly, the proliferation of distributed key-value stores has set up the ground for developing more graph-oriented RDF stores in the cloud.

Trinity.RDF [Shao et al., 2013], proposed by Microsoft, is the first system adopting a graph-oriented approach for RDF data management using cloud infrastructures. It uses as its underlying storage and indexing mechanism Trinity [Shao et al., 2013], a distributed graph system built on top of a memory key-value store. An RDF graph is distributed among the cluster machines by hashing the values of the nodes of the RDF graph (subjects and objects of RDF triples); thus, each machine holds a disjoint part of the RDF graph. Figure 3.2 depicts a possible partitioning of the RDF graph of Figure 2.2 in a cluster of two machines.

In Trinity.RDF, the RDF graph (where resources are nodes and triples are edges) is split into partitions, where each resource is assigned to a single machine. However, because some edges inevitably will traverse the partitioning, each machine will also store some such edges that are outgoing from the resources assigned to that machines. In other words, these are triples whose subject URI is part of that machine's partition, while the object URI is not.

Within each machine, the URIs (or constants) labeling the RDF graph nodes are used as keys, while two adjacency lists are stored as values: one for the incoming edges and another for the outgoing one. Using our storage description, this corresponds to an S{PO} and O{PS} index, respectively. Since these two indices do not allow retrieving triples *by the value of their property*, e.g., to match (?x, :name, ?y), Trinity.RDF comprises a separate index whose keys are the property values and whose values are two lists, one with the subjects and another with

Table 3.4: Indexing in Trinity.RDF at a two-machines cluster. Key-value store at machine 1 (left) and machine 2 (right).

Key	Value
:picasso	OUT(:paints, :guernica)
	OUT(:name,"Pablo")
:guernica	IN(:paints, :picasso)
	OUT(:exhibited,:reinasofia)
:reinasofia	IN(:exhibited, :guernica)
	OUT(:located, :madrid)
:rodin	OUT(:creates, :thethinker)
	OUT(:name,"Auguste")
:paris	IN(:located,:museerodin)
:paints	{:picasso}, {:guernica}
:name	{:picasso, :rodin}, {-}
:located	{:reinasofia}, {:paris}
:exhibited	{:guernica}, {:reinasofia}
:creates	{:rodin}, {-}

Key	Value
:marid	in(:located, :reinasofia)
:museerodin	in(:exhibited, :thethinker)
	out(:located, :paris)
:thethinker	in(:creates,:rodin)
	out(:exhibited,:museerodin)
"Pablo"	in(:name,:picasso)
"Auguste"	in(:name,:rodin)
:located	{:reinasofia}, {:madrid}
:creates	{-}, {:thethinker}
:exhibited	{:thethinker}, {:museerodin}
:name	{-}, {"Pablo","Auguste"}

the objects of each property. This approach amounts to storing the indices P{S} and P{O}, in our notation.

Table 3.4 illustrates the RDF graph partitioning of Figure 3.2 in the key-value store of Trinity. Each node in the graph is stored as a key in one of the two machines together with its incoming and outgoing edges; graph navigation is implemented by lookups on these nodes. The example shown in Table 3.4 is the simplest way of RDF indexing in Trinity, where IN and OUT denote the lists of incoming and outgoing edges, respectively. In Shao et al. [2013], the authors propose a further modification of this storage model aiming at decreasing communication costs during query processing. This is achieved by partitioning the adjacency lists of a graph node by machine so that only one message is sent to each machine regardless of the number of neighbors of that node.

Stylus [He et al., 2017] is a more recent RDF store built on top of Trinity [Shao et al., 2013]. The RDF graph is partitioned over the compute nodes using random hashing. The particularity of Stylus is its compact storage scheme based on templates. These templates are inspired by the characteristic sets proposed in Neumann and Moerkotte [2011], where the authors made the observation that in most RDF graphs the property edges exhibit a certain structure, e.g., :painters tend to have a :name and :paints property. Stylus uses a compact data structure based on user-defined types, called xUDT, to represent such groups of properties and the RDF

Table 3.5: Indexing in Stylus

Key (*gid*)	Value (list of properties)
1	:paints, :name
2	:creates, :name
3	:exhibited

Key (subject)	Value (*gid*, *offsets*, *obj_vals*)
:picasso	$1, 0, 2$, :guernica, :lareve, "Pablo"
:rodin	$2, 0, 1$, :thethinker, "Auguste"
:guernica	$3, 0$, :reinasofia
:thethinker	$3, 0$, :museerodin

triples. Each group of properties $\{:p_1, :p_2, ..., :p_n\}$ is stored in the key-value store as: $(gid, \{:p_1, :p_2, ..., :p_n\})$ where gid is an identifier of the group. Then, each RDF subject id having the group of properties gid is stored as: $(id, \{gid, \textit{offsets}, obj\_vals\})$ where obj_vals represents a list of object values of the triples having subject id and *offsets* is a list of integers specifying the offset of the object values for the properties of the current subject. Table 3.5 shows an example of Stylus storage scheme for our running example. The table on the left keeps the group of properties, while the table on the right the information for the RDF subjects.

Stylus storage scheme provides not only efficient data access but also can reduce the number of joins required to answer a query. Being also in a main-memory key-value store, it achieves great performance speed-ups. This comes at a cost of longer times for loading the input data.

3.4   STORING IN MULTIPLE CENTRALIZED RDF STORES

This category comprises systems that exploit in parallel a set of centralized RDF stores distributed among many nodes. Their goal is to benefit from the fast selective access that centralized RDF stores provide for small datasets and the low latency of parallel computation. For this reason, large RDF graphs are partitioned in smaller ones, each of them being stored in an RDF store in a separate machine.

These systems have a master/slave architecture, where the master is responsible for partitioning and placing the RDF triples in the slave nodes. Each slave node stores and indexes its local RDF triples in a centralized RDF store. The challenge is to partition the RDF data in a way that enables high parallelization during query evaluation while striving to minimize communication among the slave nodes. For this reason, in this section we focus on the different partitioning strategies used in such systems [Galarraga et al., 2012, Hose and Schenkel, 2013a, Huang et al., 2011, Lee and Liu, 2013, Wu et al., 2015].

H-RDF-3X [Huang et al., 2011] was the first work to follow this path. RDF graphs are partitioned by METIS [Karypis and Kumar, 1998], which splits the vertices of a graph into k partitions so that a minimum number of edges is cut (an edge cut occurs when the subject and

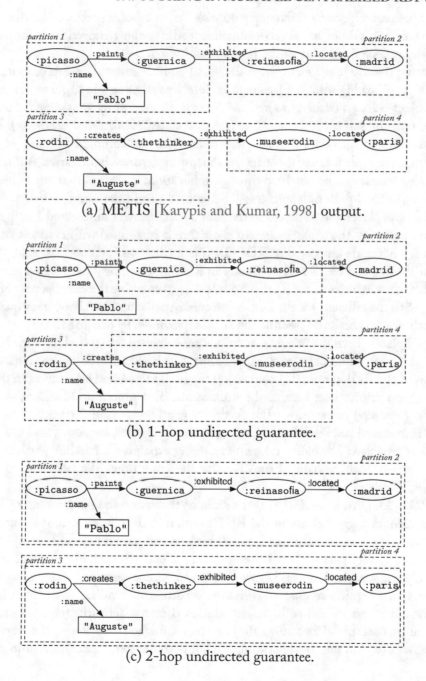

(a) METIS [Karypis and Kumar, 1998] output.

(b) 1-hop undirected guarantee.

(c) 2-hop undirected guarantee.

Figure 3.3: Partitioning and placement based on Huang et al. [2011].

object of a triple are assigned to different partitions). The number of partitions k is the number of available slave nodes. Triples whose predicate value is rdf:type are removed from the partitioning process as they reduce the quality of the graph partitioning.

Assuming that we have four nodes available, Figure 3.3 shows a possible output of METIS for the RDF graph of Figure 2.2. Placement is done by assigning the triple to the partition to which its subject belongs (referred as *directed 1-hop guarantee*) or by assigning the triple to the partitions of both its subject and the object (referred as *undirected 1-hop guarantee*). To further reduce communication network during query evaluation, the authors of Huang et al. [2011] allow for even more replication of those triples that are at partition boundaries. A *directed (undirected) n-hop guarantee* can be obtained through replication; it ensures that any triples forming a directed (undirected) path of length n will be located within the same partition. Figures 3.3 and 3.3 depict the placement of triples to the four partitions with undirected 1-hop and 2-hop guarantee, respectively. The triple placement algorithm is performed with Hadoop jobs, and the local triples at each node are stored in RDF-3X [Neumann and Weikum, 2010a].

SHAPE [Lee and Liu, 2013] partitions an RDF graph using a hash-based approach that considers also the semantics of the RDF graph. It tries to combine the effectiveness of the graph partitioning with the efficiency of the hashing to create partitions that allow many queries to run locally at each node. It starts by creating the *baseline partitions* by hashing the triples using their subject (resp. object). Then the baseline partitions are extended by: (i) hashing the objects (resp. subjects) of the triples that belong to this partition; (ii) hashing the subjects (resp. objects) of all the triples of the RDF graph; (iii) comparing the hash values, and associating to the baseline partition the new triples that hash to the same value. This procedure is known as *1-forward* (respectively, *1-reverse*) *partitioning*. The partitions can be extended further, following the k-hop notion introduced in H-RDF-3X, leading to the *k-forward*, *k-reverse*, and *k-bidirectional* partitioning approaches. The bidirectional partitioning expands the baseline partition using the hash of the subject and the hash of the object at the same time. The partitions are stored in centralized RDF stores.

PP-RDF-3X [Wu et al., 2015] is the state of the art on the partitioning of large RDF graphs. The authors suggest dividing the RDF graph into disjoint partitions using *end-to-end paths* as the smallest partition element (a single end-to-end path must reside completely inside a partition). Thus, every partition can be seen as a set of end-to-end paths. An end-to-end path can be roughly characterized as a *maximum-length path from a source node to a sink node.*[2] Setting up the store, then, requires finding all end-to-end paths and dividing them into disjoint sets. Since two or more end-to-end paths might contain common subpaths (common triples), the authors develop a cost model for finding the best trade-off when partitioning the graph, between replicating nodes (which improves performance but occupies more space) and disjointness. The

---

[2]The exact definition is a bit more involved, allowing for directed cycles to occur in specific places with respect to the end-to-end path, in particular at the end; a sample end-to-end path is $u_1, u_2, u_3, u_4, u_5, u_3$, for some u_i URIs in the RDF graph, $1 \leq i \leq 5$.

problem is NP-Hard, thus they propose an approximate algorithm for solving it. Similar to SHAPE and H-RDF-3X, they store the derived partitions in local RDF-3X stores.

In Wu et al. [2012], HadoopDB [Abouzeid et al., 2009] is used, where RDF triples are stored in a DBMS at each node. Triples are stored using the vertical partitioning proposed in Abadi et al. [2007], i.e., one table with two columns per property. Triple placement is decided by hashing the subjects and/or objects of the triples according to how the properties are connected in the RDF Schema. If the RDF Schema is not available, a schema is built by analyzing the data at loading time.

DREAM [Hammoud et al., 2015] proposes to replicate the entire RDF graph to all compute nodes with the assumption that the graph fits in the compute nodes. The benefit of this approach is that there is no preprocessing (partitioning) cost when storing the data as well as reducing the communication cost. DREAM uses RDF-3X in each node to store the RDF graph.

Finally, gStoreD [Peng et al., 2016b] stores each partition of the RDF graph in a local gStore instance. gStore [Zou et al., 2011] is a centralized graph-based RDF store which uses the typical adjacency list representation for storing RDF graphs backed by structural indices capable of pruning large parts of the dataset. gStoreD is oblivious to the partitioning strategy of the RDF graph and, thus, one can partition the RDF graph in any way. This is thanks to their "partial evaluation and assembly" query evaluation strategy, as we will discuss in the next chapter.

Workload-Based

There are a few works that take a query workload into consideration for determining the best partitioning strategy.

WARP [Hose and Schenkel, 2013a] extends the partitioning and replication techniques of Huang et al. [2011] to take into account a query workload in order to choose the parts of RDF data that need to be replicated. Thus, rarely used RDF data does not need to be replicated, leading to a reduced storage overhead compared to the one of Huang et al. [2011].

Partout [Galarraga et al., 2012] is a distributed RDF engine also concerned with partitioning RDF, inspired by a query workload, so that queries are processed over a minimum number of nodes. The partitioning process is split in two tasks: fragmentation, i.e., split the triples into pieces, and fragment allocation, i.e., in which node each piece will be stored. The fragmentation is based on a horizontal partitioning of the triple relation based on the set of constants appearing in the queries, while the fragment allocation is done so that most of the queries can be executed locally at one host but at the same time maintaining load balancing. This is done by looking for the number of queries for each fragment that need to access it as well as the number of triples required for such query. The triple partitioning process takes into consideration load imbalances and space constraints to assign the partitions to the available nodes.

In Peng et al. [2016a] the authors first mine patterns from the workload with high-access frequencies. Then, based on these frequent access patterns, they propose two different partitioning policies: one that stores the RDF subgraph that matches a frequent access pattern as a whole in one compute node (vertical partitioning) and one that splits the RDF subgraph that matches a frequent access pattern and stores it in different compute nodes (horizontal partitioning). In the vertical partitioning, when a query that contains a frequent access pattern arrives, it will typically be evaluated locally on only one compute node. In this way, multiple compute nodes can be used to evaluate multiple queries simultaneously. While the vertical partitioning policy improves query response time as well as query throughput due to its local evaluation, the horizontal partitioning can improve query response time due to its high parallelism.

3.5 STORING IN MAIN MEMORY STORES

Storing RDF in main memory appeared very early in the Semantic Web community with many supporters like Redland [Beckett, 2001], RDFSuite [Alexaki et al., 2000, 2001], Jena [McBride, 2002], and Sesame [Broekstra et al., 2002]. Over the years this approach was abandoned since the large amount of RDF data could not fit anymore in the main memory of a centralized system. Currently, with the price consistently dropping and the wide adoption of cloud solutions, this approach has come back into fashion.

Trinity.RDF [Shao et al., 2013], discussed in Section 3.3, is the first distributed RDF system storing data in the main memory indirectly by exploiting an in-memory key-value store. TriAD [Gurajada et al., 2014] is the main representative of a distributed in-memory RDF data management system. It combines and extends various techniques that lead to efficient RDF query processing. Similar to H-RDF-3X, it employs a graph partition strategy using the METIS graph partitioner [Karypis and Kumar, 1998] to divide the original RDF dataset into partitions. Based on the METIS result, it builds a summary graph used to restrict query processing to only its interesting part before evaluating the query. Every triple is replicated to two partitions using the subject and the object. Then, for every subject partition, it builds the indexes $\overrightarrow{SPO}$, $\overrightarrow{SOP}$, and $\overrightarrow{PSO}$, and for every object partition it builds the indexes $\overrightarrow{OSP}$, $\overrightarrow{OPS}$, and $\overrightarrow{POS}$. The indexes are sorted in lexicographic order and are stored in main memory. TriAD holds statistics for every possible combination of S, P, and O from the data graph and the summary graph.

Finally, TensorRDF [Virgilio, 2017] is implemented in the message passing interface (MPI) and uses the Lustre file system, an in-memory file system for MPI programs. It stores RDF triples in rank-3 tensors by first mapping elements of RDF triples to natural numbers. Thus, the (ijk) element of the tensor is equal to 1 if and only if the triple i j k exists. As the tensor is very sparse (contains many zero values), the authors use the Coordinate Sparse Tensors (CST) format to store the data. This format keeps only a list of all non-zero entries describing the coordinates and the value, e.g., $\{i, j, k\} \to 1$. The CST data structure is then simply distributed evenly among the processes, thanks to the associative and distributive properties of linear forms.

3.6   STORING IN MULTIPLE BACK-END STORES

In the third category, we classify systems which exploit a combination of a distributed file system, a key-value store, and a centralized RDF store. Such a system is AMADA [Aranda-Andújar et al., 2012, Bugiotti et al., 2012, 2014], which is built upon services provided by commercial clouds. In AMADA, RDF data is stored in a distributed file system, and the focus is on efficiently routing queries to only those datasets that are likely to have matches for the query. Selective query routing reduces the total work associated with processing a query; in a cloud environment, this also translates into financial cost savings. Thus, AMADA takes advantage of: large-scale stores for the data itself; the fine-grained search capabilities of a fast key-value store for efficient query routing, and an out-of-the-box centralized RDF store for caching relative datasets and efficiently answer queries.

AMADA stores RDF datasets within Amazon's Simple Storage Service (S3), a distributed file system for raw (file) storage. Then, indices are built in Amazon's key-value store, DynamoDB [Dynamo]. These indices differ from the ones in Section 3.3 because they are used for mapping RDF elements to the RDF graphs containing them and not for indexing RDF triples themselves. For example, using the storage description grammar (Definition 3.1), the index S{G} shows which subject values S can be found in which RDF graphs G. Similar indices are used for property and object values or a combination of them. In Bugiotti et al. [2014] the following indexing schemes are proposed and experimentally compared:

- term-based indexing, which uses the index T{G}, where T is any RDF term regardless of its position;

- attribute-based indexing, which uses three indices: S{G}, P{G}, O{G}; and

- attribute-subset indexing, which uses seven indices: S{G}, P{G}, O{G}, SP{G}, PO{G}, SO{G}, SPO{G}.

The indices outlined above enable efficient query processing in AMADA through routing incoming queries (only) to those graphs that may have useful results, as we explain in Chapter 4. These datasets are then loaded in a centralized RDF store.

3.7   SUMMARY

Table 3.6 summarizes the back-end and storage layout schemes used by the RDF stores. For each, we also present the benefit of its chosen storage scheme, outlining three classes of back-ends used for storing RDF triples: distributed file systems, key-value stores, and centralized RDF stores.

We observe that almost all systems based on a key-value store adopt a three-indices scheme, and specifically the indices SPO, POS, and OSP. Only Trinity.RDF [Shao et al., 2013] adopts a slightly different indexing scheme, with a second-level index as described above. Finally,

Table 3.6: Comparison of storage schemes. Storage systems used: DFS=Distributed file system, KVS=Key-value store, CS=Centralized store, MS=Memory store. (*Continues.*)

System	Storage	Partitioning Description	Benefit
SHARD [Rohloff and Schantz, 2010]	DFS	CP(S){PO}	Simplified storage
PigSPARQL [Schätzle et al., 2011]	DFS	CP(*)	Simplified storage
HadoopRDF [Husain et al., 2011]	DFS	HP(P){SO}	Reduce I/O and data processing
RAPID+ [Kim et al., 2011; Ravindra et al., 2011]	DFS	HP(P){SO}	Reduce I/O and data processing
[Zhang et al., 2012]	DFS	HP(P){SO}	Reduce I/O and data processing
EAGRE [Zhang et al., 2013]	DFS	S{PO}, compressed entity graph partitioning	Reduce I/O and data processing
CliqueSquare [Goasdoue et al., 2015]	DFS	HP(S){PO}, HP(P){SO}, HP(O){SP}	Reduce I/O and data processing
S2RDF [Schätzle et al., 2016]	DFS	HP(P){SO} + semi-join reductions	Reduce I/O and data processing
H$_2$RDF [Papailiou et al., 2012]	KVS	$\overrightarrow{SP}${O}, $\overrightarrow{PO}${S}, $\overrightarrow{OS}${P}	Fast data access
H$_2$RDF+ [Papailiou et al., 2013]	KVS	$\overrightarrow{SPO}$, $\overrightarrow{POS}$, $\overrightarrow{OSP}$, $\overrightarrow{SOP}$, $\overrightarrow{PSO}$, $\overrightarrow{OPS}$	Fast data access
Rya [Punnoose et al., 2012]	KVS	$\overline{SPO}$, $\overline{POS}$, $\overline{OSP}$	Fast data access
AMADA [Aranda-Andújar et al., 2012; Bugiotti et al., 2012, 2014]	KVS	S{P{O}}, P{O{S}}, O{S{P}}	Fast data access
MAPSIN [Przyjaciel-Zablocki et al., 2012]	KVS	$\overrightarrow{S}$ {P{O}}, $\overrightarrow{O}$ {S{P}}	Fast data access
Stratustore [Stein and Zacharias, 2010b]	KVS	S{P{O}}	Fast data access
CumulusRDF-hierarchical [Ladwig and Harth, 2011]	KVS	S{P{O}}, P{O{S}}, O{S{P}}	Fast data access
CumulusRDF-flat [Ladwig and Harth, 2011]	KVS	S{PO}, PO{S}, O{SP}, PO{P̲{P}}, P{PO}	Fast data access

Table 3.6: (*Continued.*) Comparison of storage schemes. Storage systems used: DFS=Distributed file system, KVS=Key-value store, CS=Centralized store, MS=Memory store.

Trinity.RDF [Shao et al., 2013]	KVS	S{PO}, O{PS}, P{S}, P{O}	Fast data access
Stylus [He et al., 2017]	KVS	HP(S){PO}	Fast data access and join reduction
H-RDF-3X [Huang et al., 2011]	CS	GP(*){$\overrightarrow{SPO}$}, GP(*){$\overrightarrow{POS}$}, GP(*){$\overrightarrow{OSP}$}, GP(*){$\overrightarrow{SOP}$}, GP(*){$\overrightarrow{PSO}$}, GP(*){$\overrightarrow{OPS}$}	Reduce communication cost
WARP [Hose and Schenkel, 2013a]	CS	GP(*){$\overrightarrow{SPO}$}, GP(*){$\overrightarrow{POS}$}, GP(*){$\overrightarrow{OSP}$}, GP(*){$\overrightarrow{SOP}$}, GP(*){$\overrightarrow{PSO}$}, GP(*){$\overrightarrow{OPS}$}	Reduce communication cost
Partout [Galarraga et al., 2012]	CS	Horizontal fragmentation based on query workload	Reduce communication cost
SHAPE [Lee and Liu, 2013]	CS	HP(*){$\overrightarrow{SPO}$}, HP(*){$\overrightarrow{POS}$}, HP(*){$\overrightarrow{OSP}$}, HP(*){$\overrightarrow{SOP}$}, HP(*){$\overrightarrow{PSO}$}, HP(*){$\overrightarrow{OPS}$}	Reduce communication cost
PP-RDF-3X [Wu et al., 2015]	CS	GP(*){$\overrightarrow{SPO}$}, GP(*){$\overrightarrow{POS}$}, GP(*){$\overrightarrow{OSP}$}, GP(*){$\overrightarrow{SOP}$}, GP(*){$\overrightarrow{PSO}$}, GP(*){$\overrightarrow{OPS}$}	Reduce communication cost
DREAM [Hammoud et al., 2015]	CS	None	Reduce communication cost
gStoreD [Peng et al., 2016b]	CS	Any	Reduce communication cost
TriAD [Gurajada et al., 2014]	MS	GP(*){$\overrightarrow{SPO}$}, GP(*){$\overrightarrow{POS}$}, GP(*){$\overrightarrow{OSP}$}, GP(*){$\overrightarrow{SOP}$}, GP(*){$\overrightarrow{PSO}$}, GP(*){$\overrightarrow{OPS}$}	Fast data access
TensorRDF [Virgilio, 2017]	MS	CP{SPO}, tensorial format	Fast parallel data access

the only works that consider a query workload for the partitioning process are WARP [Hose and Schenkel, 2013a] and Partout [Galarraga et al., 2012].

An experimental study of the various partitioning techniques for both centralized and distributed RDF stores can be found in Abdelaziz et al. [2017a]. Their results show that there is no clear winner, i.e., no partitioning algorithm fits all datasets and query types. The complexity of sophisticated partitioning schemes does not allow distributed RDF stores to process very large RDF datasets in a reasonable amount of time. At the same time, they do not always ensure better query performance compared to simple partitioning strategies. For example, MapReduce-based systems suffer from the overhead of uploading data on HDFS first before partitioning, while systems using METIS for partitioning have significant preprocessing cost since METIS cannot scale to large RDF graphs [Lee and Liu, 2013]. They also conclude that TriAD provides the lowest storage and partitioning overhead among their evaluated systems. However, it has a huge memory overhead because it keeps the whole RDF graph in memory.

CHAPTER 4

Cloud-Based SPARQL Query Processing

A second very important aspect of RDF data management is query processing: given a query, how the system evaluates it to return the complete answer. In this chapter, we describe how cloud-based RDF systems process SPARQL queries, usually in a parallel manner. There are two main directions of works on the query processing dimension. The first class of works are based on well-known relational techniques, which we present in Section 4.1. The second class of works is based on graph exploration techniques based on the graph structure of the data which we present in Section 4.2. While there are only a few works that use graph techniques, there are plentiful works based on relational processing strategies.

We split all works in two dimensions: data access paths (Section 4.1.1) and join evaluation (Section 4.1.2). The data access paths determine how the triple patterns of the SPARQL queries are matched (e.g., if there are indices), and they strongly depend on where the storage the data resides. The join evaluation dimension determines how the intermediate results are joined (e.g., if they are evaluated in MapReduce, which join algorithms are used, etc.).

Throughout this chapter we will use as our running example the SPARQL query shown below (Figure 4.1). The query asks for the artists' paintings which are exhibited in museums located in Paris.

4.1 RELATIONAL-BASED QUERY PROCESSING

From a database perspective, two are the core operations in evaluating a SPARQL query:

- triple pattern matching, which finds all the triples (potentially from several storage nodes) matching a certain triple pattern; and

- n-ary join, for some $n \geq 2$, in which several inputs are joined on a set of common variables. Given that each variable corresponds to a triple subject or object (most frequently) or property (less often), the joins serve to "stitch" together partial query results toward building full query answers.

Works in this category can be classified according to the taxonomy of Figure 4.2. In the following, we first discuss the data access paths strategies for evaluating triple pattern scans, and then dive into the join evaluation.

```
SELECT ?y ?z
WHERE {
?x :type :artist .
?x :paints ?y .
?y :exhibited ?z .
?z :located :paris . }
```

Figure 4.1: Running example of SPARQL query.

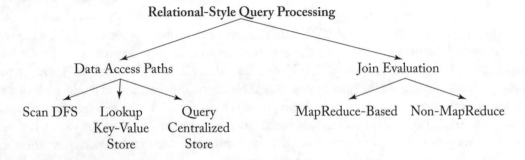

Figure 4.2: Taxonomy of relational-style query processing strategies.

4.1.1 DATA ACCESS PATHS

Data access paths of query evaluation are tightly coupled with the underlying storage facility. We categorize them accordingly.

Distributed File Systems

When RDF data is stored in a distributed file system, scanning is the only feasible way to select the triples that match a given triple pattern since no indices are provided.

In systems that store RDF data according to the triple model described in Section 3.2.1, all the files are scanned and a selection operation is performed to match the triple pattern. In Rohloff and Schantz [2010] and Schätzle et al. [2011], the selection is performed in the map phase of the corresponding MapReduce job.

In systems based on the vertical partitioning (Section 3.2.2), triple pattern matching is performed by selecting the files named after the property of the triple pattern. If the subject and/or object of the triple pattern is also constant (specified by the query), the corresponding selection conditions are enforced on the data retrieved from those files. In Goasdoué et al. [2015], Husain et al. [2011], Ravindra et al. [2011], Schätzle et al. [2016], and Zhang et al. [2012], the selection is performed in the corresponding map phase. As in the case of centralized stores, this kind of partitioning works well in the cases of triple patterns with a bound predicate. Such triple atoms appear to be very frequent in real-world SPARQL queries, amounting to about 78% of the DBPedia query log and 99.47% of the Semantic Web Dog query log, according to Arias et al. [2011]. However, when the property attribute of a triple pattern is unbound, all files residing in the DFS need to be scanned.

An interesting aspect of HadoopRDF [Husain et al., 2011] and Cliquesquare [Goasdoué et al., 2015] is that data access enables query minimization during the file selection process. For a triple pattern $t_1 = (s_1, p_1, o_1)$ where p_1 is distinct from :type and o_1 a variable, HadoopRDF checks if the type of the object is specified by another triple pattern $t_2 = (o_1, :type, o_2)$ in the query. If this is the case, the selected file is only $p_1 \# o_2$, and t_2 is removed from the query. Otherwise, all files prefixed with p_1 are selected.

In EAGRE [Zhang et al., 2013], a distributed I/O scheduling solution is proposed for reducing the I/O cost incurred before the filtering of the map phase, especially for queries with range and order constraints. Query evaluation is postponed until the I/O scheduling has determined which are the data blocks that contain answers to a given query (and thus, need to be scanned).

Key Value Stores

When RDF triples are stored in a key-value store, triple pattern matching becomes more efficient due to the indexing capabilities.

Access paths depend on the way RDF data is indexed in the key-value store and the kind of index the underlying key-value store supports (hash- or sorted index). If it is a hash index, a direct lookup is necessary to retrieve the values of a given key; in contrast, if it is a sorted index, a prefix lookup is also possible. In some cases, post-processing is required after the lookup to further filter out triples which do not match the triple pattern.

Table 4.1 shows the access paths provided by each such system for each possible query triple pattern template. We denote by $DL(T)$ a direct lookup to a table T, by $PL(T)$ a prefix lookup, and by $S(T)$ a scan over the whole table T. In addition, we use *csel* to denote that an extra selection operation is required at the client side, while *ssel* specifies when the selection can be performed on the server side (where the key-value store is located). For the case of Stratustore where SimpleDB is used, there is also the possibility of SELECT queries which return keys and values by specifying the columns. We denote such cases by $SDB(T)$.

For a boolean triple pattern (all its elements are constants) a direct lookup to any of the available tables can be performed, and then (depending on the indexing strategy) a selection may be needed. Similarly, for a variable-only triple pattern, a scan over any of the available tables is suitable. For the remaining possible combinations of variables, constants, and URIs in triple patterns, we may need to perform either a direct lookup, or a direct lookup with some post-filtering, or a prefix lookup.

Hybrid Approaches

An alternative approach is presented in AMADA [Aranda-Andújar et al., 2012, Bugiotti et al., 2012, 2014], where data resides in a cloud store and indices are kept in a key-value store.

Table 4.1: Triple pattern access paths in key-value stores

Triple Pattern	Rya	H2RDF	AMADA	MAPSIN	Stratustore	CumulusRDF Hierarchical	CumulusRDF Flat
(s, p, o)	$DL(*)$	$DL(*)+csel$	$DL(*)+csel$	$DL(*)+ssel$	$DL(*)+csel$	$DL(*)+csel$	$DL(*)+csel$
$(s, p, ?o)$	$PL(SPO)$	$DL(SP|O)$	$DL(S|P|O)+csel$	$DL(S|P|O)+ssel$	$DL(S|P|O)+csel$	$2\times DL(S|\{P\}O)+csel$	$DL(S|\{P\}O|\epsilon)$ $DL+PL(S|PO|\epsilon)$
$(s, ?p, o)$	$PL(OSP)$	$DL(OS|P)$	$DL(O|S|P)+csel$	$DL(O|S|P)+ssel$	$DL(S|P|O)+csel$	$2\times DL(O|\{S\}P)+csel$	$DL+PL(O|SP|\epsilon)$
$(s, ?p, ?o)$	$PL(SPO)$	$PL(SP|O)$	$DL(S|P|O)$	$DL(S|P|O)$	$DL(S|P|O)$	$DL(S|\{P\}O|\epsilon)$	$DL(S|PO|\epsilon)$
$(?s, p, o)$	$PL(POS)$	$DL(PO|S)$	$DL(P|O|S)$	$DL(O|S|P)+ssel$	$SDB(S|P|O)$	$DL(P|\{O\}S|\epsilon)$	$DL(PO|S|\epsilon)$
$(?s, p, ?o)$	$PL(POS)$	$PL(PO|S)$	$DL(P|O|S)$	$S(*)+ssel$	$SDB(S|P|O)$	$DL(P|\{O\}S|\epsilon)$	$DL(PO|\{P\}P)+$ $DL(PO|S|\epsilon)$
$(?s, ?p, o)$	$PL(OSP)$	$PL(OS|P)$	$DL(O|S|P)$	$DL(O|S|P)$	$S(*)+csel$	$DL(O|\{S\}P|\epsilon)$	$DL(O|SP|\epsilon)$
$(?s, ?p, ?o)$	$S(*)$	$S(*)$	$S(*)$	$S(*)$	$S(*)$	$S(*)$	$S(*)$

Query processing is achieved by selecting a (hopefully tight) superset of the RDF datasets which contain answers to a given query. This is done by advising the available indices (see Section 3.6). Then, the selected RDF datasets are loaded at query time in a centralized state-of-the-art RDF store which gives the answer to the query.

In-Memory Distributed RDF Stores

Recall that TriaD [Gurajada et al., 2014] creates six in-memory indices in each compute node, one for each SPO permutation. Thus, for each triple-pattern, TriaD invokes a parallel index scan of a permutation index depending on the constants of the triple pattern. On the contrary, TensorRDF [Virgilio, 2017][1] matches a triple pattern by employing the Kroneker delta in tensor calculus. The Kroneker delta is a function which takes as input two numerical variables and returns 1 if the variables are equal and 0 otherwise.

Federated Centralized RDF Stores

Huang et al. [2011] and WARP [Hose and Schenkel, 2013b] aim at pushing as much as possible query processing to the centralized RDF stores which have been proved to be very efficient. After the SPARQL query has been decomposed into a set of subqueries, data accessed is implemented by sending each subquery to all instances of RDF store in parallel. This is necessary since there is no index to map the data to the partitions it belongs. For instance, if the undirected 2-hop guarantee of Huang et al. [2011] is provided by the store (Figure 3.3), the query of Figure 4.1 can be evaluated by sending it to all four partitions. If a query cannot be completely answered from the underlying store, further joins are required to recombine the subquery results, as we explain in the next section.

While Hose and Schenkel [2013b] and Huang et al. [2011] lack indexes for routing the subqueries to the partitions containing results, Partout [Galarraga et al., 2012] identifies the nodes that are relevant to a specific triple pattern at the coordinator node, which keeps mappings of terms appearing in the query workload to nodes when the partitioning process takes place.

All these three works use RDF-3X [Neumann and Weikum, 2010a] as the underlying store at each partition, and as a consequence, a local index of all possible orders and combinations of triple elements enables efficient local data access at the granularity of triple patterns.

4.1.2   JOIN EVALUATION

Joins are at the core of SPARQL query evaluation. Typical SPARQL queries require the evaluation of many join operators. For example, for the query in Figure 4.1, we have one join on variable ?x between the first and second triple patterns, one join on variable ?y between the second and third triple patterns, and one join on variable ?z between the third and fourth triple patterns. In this section, we will discuss the type of join implementations that different systems

---

[1]Even though TensorRDF is not explicitly relational-based, its tensor calculus operations naturally match the relational model operations.

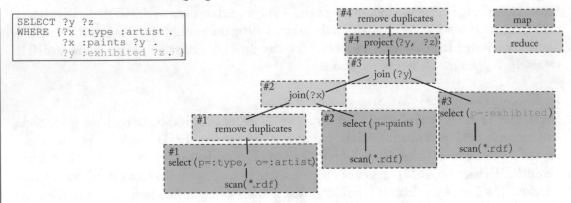

Figure 4.3: MapReduce join evaluation in SHARD based on Rohloff and Schantz [2010].

use, i.e., the physical operators. We discuss the order in which these joins can be executed in the next chapter.

Join evaluation is a challenging problem in cloud-based RDF systems because neither key-value stores nor MapReduce inherently support joins. For this reason, very early works on indexing RDF in key-value stores do not handle joins, such as CumulusRDF [Ladwig and Harth, 2011] which supports only single triple-pattern queries. Among the rest of systems, there is a large amount of works that use MapReduce to evaluate joins. For this reason, in the following, we distinguish between works that use MapReduce-based joins and works that perform join evaluation out of MapReduce, often at a single site.

MapReduce-Based Joins
The first system to use MapReduce for SPARQL query evaluation is SHARD [Rohloff and Schantz, 2010]. In SHARD, one MapReduce job is initialized for each triple pattern. In addition, a last job is created for removing redundant results (if necessary) and outputting the corresponding values for the variables that need to be projected. In the map phase of each job, the triples that match the triple pattern are sent to the reducers. In the reduce phase, the matched triples are joined with the intermediate results of the previous triple patterns (if any). Figure 4.3 illustrates the join evaluation using a SPARQL query with the three of the triple patterns of the running example of Figure 4.1. Conceptually, SHARD's query evaluation strategy leads to left-deep query plans, which are often used in traditional centralized databases. We discuss about different query plans in the next chapter. Note that for a three-triple pattern query, four jobs are required, while all data is scanned three times. This leads to much I/O overhead. Subsequent works aim at improving this overhead.

In Schätzle et al. [2011] the authors propose a mapping from full SPARQL 1.0 to Pig Latin [Olston et al., 2008], a higher level language of MapReduce which provides higher-level primitives such as filters, joins, and unions. Each triple pattern is transformed to a Pig Latin

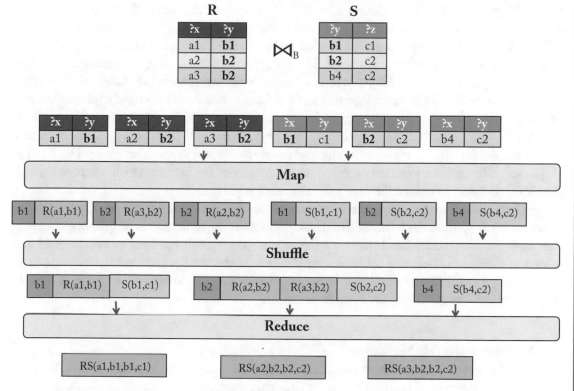

Figure 4.4: Repartition join in MapReduce.

filter operation, while the triple patterns are successively joined one after the other; Left-outer joins and unions are also used for more complex SPARQL queries, like ones with OPTIONAL and UNION expressions. The way the joins are implemented and any other implementation issue is left to the Apache Pig system.[2]

HadoopRDF uses a hash-based repartition join [Blanas et al., 2010]. Figure 4.4 illustrates this type of join on two relations R and S. The columns are variables of a SPARQL query and the join is on variable $?y$. Cliquesquare uses the hash-based repartition join when joining intermediate results. When joining triple patterns, data is co-partitioned thanks to its partitioning scheme. For this reason, Cliquesquare uses a Map-join where hash joins happen locally at the map phase.

Although H_2RDF+ stores the RDF data in a key-value store, it uses MapReduce query plans to evaluate queries which have been predicted to be non-selective, and thus, benefit from parallelization of processing of a big amount of data. H2RDF+ [Papailiou et al., 2013] takes advantage of the indices kept in HBase and, when joining triple patterns, it uses a merge join

[2]https://pig.apache.org/

with a Map-only job. When joining a triple pattern with intermediate results (which are not sorted), it uses a sort-merge join. In case both relations to be joined are intermediate results, it falls back to the hash-based repartition join. In Przyjaciel-Zablocki et al. [2012], a Map-side index nested loops algorithm is proposed for joining triple patterns. The join between two triple patterns is computed in the Map-phase of a job by retrieving values that match the first triple pattern from the key-value store, injecting each of these values into the second triple pattern and performing the corresponding lookup for the second pattern in the key-value store. No shuffle or reduce phases are required. As an optimization, the triple patterns that share a common variable on the subject (or object) are grouped and evaluated at once in a single Map phase. In Zhang et al. [2012], Bloom filter joins are executed whenever one of the input is small/selective enough that it can be used to reduce the data from the other inputs.

Note that there has been extensive research on different types of relational joins (theta-joins, equi-joins, similarity joins, etc.) and how they can be implemented in MapReduce. Among the most popular techniques is the repartition join, where both relations get partitioned and joined in different nodes, and the broadcast join, where the smallest relation is broadcast to all nodes and joined with the partitions of the larger relation. The interested reader may refer to this survey in Li et al. [2014] for more information.

Join Evaluation Outside MapReduce

Systems that execute joins outside MapReduce store their data (i) in key-value stores, (ii) centralized RDF stores over multiple nodes, or (iii) main memory.

In the first category, systems typically implement their own join operators, since key-value stores do not allow for operations across tables (e.g., joins). Often the evaluation of SPARQL queries in such systems is done *locally* at a single site, outside of the key-value store. For each triple pattern, the appropriate lookups are performed on the right tables of the key-value store, and then the results are joined to produce the final answer.

Rya [Crainiceanu et al., 2012] implements an index nested-loops algorithm using multiple lookups in the key-value store, similar to Przyjaciel-Zablocki et al. [2012] but without using MapReduce. For the first triple pattern t_1, a lookup is performed to find bindings to its variables. Then, for the rest, triple patterns t_i, the k values from triple pattern t_{i-1} are used to rewrite t_i. Then k lookups are performed in the key-value store for t_i. This procedure is performed locally at the server side. In AMADA [Aranda-Andújar et al., 2012], a query with n triple patterns entails n lookups, whose results are joined locally using an in-house memory-hash join.

An interesting case is H$_2$RDF+ [Papailiou et al., 2013], which uses MapReduce only for the non-selective queries. For selective queries, a centralized index nested-loops algorithm is used, similar to Rya. Stratustore [Stein and Zacharias, 2010a] makes a lookup for each star-join and then performs the join among them locally.

Systems using centralized RDF stores over multiple nodes also implement their own join operators for joining the intermediary results of subqueries evaluated by the RDF store when necessary. For instance, in Hose and Schenkel [2013b], for queries that cannot be evaluated completely independently at each partition, the intermediary results from each partition are gathered in the coordinator node where the joins are performed in a left-deep query plan fashion.

In Partout [Galarraga et al., 2012], the coordinator is responsible for generating a query plan whose leaves are index scans of triple patterns at the nodes containing relevant data. Because data is stored in RDF-3X, results of the index scans are ordered, and thus, the inner operations are merge joins whenever both inputs are ordered on the join attribute. If this is not the case, the inputs need to be sorted, or a hash join is used instead. A join operator is executed at one of the nodes of its children following the optimizer's decision.

In TriaD [Gurajada et al., 2014], which is an MPI-based in-memory system, an asynchronous query plan evaluation is used in contrast to MapReduce-based systems. It uses graph summarization in the master node to reduce the scanning of the RDF data for matching triple patterns at the slave nodes. In TriaD, two different join operators are used. The first one is a distributed merge join which is used when both relations are sorted (e.g., both inputs come from the permutation indices which are sorted). The other type of join is a distributed hash join if any of the input relation is not sorted. Both join operators require data shuffling for computing the join result.

Finally, TensorRDF [Virgilio, 2017] joins two triple patterns by applying the Hadamard product (element-wise multiplication) on the results of their triple-pattern matching. The underlying framework is responsible for parallelizing the processes.

4.2   GRAPH-BASED QUERY PROCESSING

Works in this category include graph exploration and partial evaluation techniques. The former traverse the graph to form the answer to the query, while in the latter, each compute node receives the entire query, evaluates it using its local RDF fragment, and then the results are put together.

4.2.1   GRAPH EXPLORATION

Works in this category include Trinity.RDF [Zeng et al., 2013] which is built on top of the Trinity graph engine, and Spartex [Abdelaziz et al., 2015, 2017b], built on top of GPS [Salihoglu and Widom, 2013], an open source Pregel-like [Malewicz et al., 2009] system. Both Trinity.RDF and Spartex use graph exploration instead of relational-style joins in order to evaluate SPARQL queries.

Data Access Paths

In Trinity.RDF, graph exploration needs a constant subject or object (source value) to start with to match triple patterns. The node that contains the source value can easily be found through hashing. Then, the node storing the source value retrieves the nodes responsible of storing the target (object, or subject) values and sends these nodes a message. For example, assume the graph partitioning shown in Figure 3.2 and the triple pattern (:picasso, ?p, ?o). A message is first

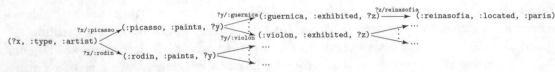

Figure 4.5: Graph exploration in Trinity.RDF for query in Figure 4.1.

sent to node 1 to determine the nodes holding the object values :picasso; in our example, these are nodes 1 and 2. From node 1 we retrieve the object value :guernica, while a message is sent to node 2, where the object value ``Pablo" is found.

If neither of the subject or object of the triple pattern are constants, the POS index is used to find matches for the given property. Graph exploration starts in parallel from each subject (or object) found and by filtering out the target values not matching the property value. If the predicate is also unbound, then every predicate is retrieved from the POS index. For example, assume again Figure 3.2 and the triple pattern (?s, :name, ?o). From the POS index (see Table 3.4), two subject values are found: :picasso and :rodin. For both of these values, the above procedure is again followed; moreover, the object values :guernica and :thinker are filtered out because the property value is not matched.

Similarly, Spartex [Abdelaziz et al., 2017b] utilizes its per-vertex two index structures (PS and PO). Given a property (edge), all nodes of the graph check their indices to extract the subjects or objects of triples having this property value.

Join Evaluation

Join evaluation in most graph-based systems is done through graph exploration. For conjunctive queries, triple patterns are processed sequentially: One triple pattern is picked as the root and a chain of triple patterns is formed. The results of each triple pattern guide the exploration of the graph for the next one. This completely avoids manipulating triple patterns that may match a triple but do not match another one considered previously during query evaluation. Figure 4.5 illustrates how the query of Figure 4.1 is processed in Trinity.RDF, assuming the given triple pattern evaluation order. Spartex works similarly in joining the triple patterns.

This graph exploration resembles the nested indexed loop join algorithm also used in Rya [Crainiceanu et al., 2012] and H_2RDF [Papailiou et al., 2012], with the difference that only the matches of the immediate neighbors of a triple pattern are kept and not all the history of the triple patterns' matches during the graph exploration, and thus, invalid results may be included in the results. For this reason, a final join is required at the end of the process to remove any invalid results that have not been pruned through the graph exploration. This join typically involves a negligible overhead.

A different approach is followed in Peng et al. [2016b] and Stylus [He et al., 2017]. They use a "partial evaluation and assembly." It sends the entire query plan to all compute nodes;

each node executes the plan and sends back the partial results to the coordinator; finally, the coordinator gathers all partial results and computes the final result.

4.2.2 PARTIAL EVALUATION AND ASSEMBLY METHODS

Novel algorithms for querying distributed graphs have been proposed in Fan et al. [2012]. The authors consider reachability queries, i.e., determining if a certain node in a fragment of a large graph is reachable from another, potentially residing on a different fragment; they consider such simple boolean reachability questions, as well as a bounded-distance version (is the node reachable by a path of at most n edges?) and a regular path version (is the node reachable by a path matching a given regular path expression?). The authors provide algorithms for answering such queries based on *partial evaluation*, where on each site, the query is evaluated based on the fragment available at that site, and partial results consist of boolean equations stating the conditions that must be met on the other (unseen) fragments in order for a partial match on this fragment to be part of a complete match. A complete match then is built by solving the system of boolean equations returned by all the sites storing fragments. The authors' algorithms provide strong performance guarantees in this setting: Each site is visited only once during query processing; the network traffic only depends on the query size and number of fragments, not on the data size; and the response time is determined by the largest fragment.

This partial evaluation approach is generalized in Peng et al. [2016b] for the evaluation of SPARQL queries, with a main focus on conjunctive BGPs. As in [Fan et al., 2012], partial matches are computed on each fragment; however, partial results now consist of tuples of nodes from the fragment which have edges connecting them to nodes from other fragments; such partial matches are put together in the assembly phase. In Peng et al. [2016b], the authors propose two assembly strategies: a centralized, where all local partial results are sent to a single compute node, and a distributed one, where a Bulk Synchronous Parallel [Valiant, 1990] model is used. The approach is quite general, as it can accommodate any graph partitioning, and builds results out of partial matches regardless of how they assemble together into global ones.

A similar approach is used by Stylus [He et al., 2017], which is built on top of the Trinity graph engine. It sends the query plan to all compute nodes; each node executes the plan and sends back the partial results, and the coordinator gathers all partial results and computes the final result.

4.3 SUMMARY

Table 4.2 summarizes the query processing strategy of each of the presented systems. In contrast to the storage-based categorization of the existing systems, where each fit in only one category, the query-based classification is less clear cut, with some systems pertaining to more than one class. For example, H_2RDF uses both a MapReduce-based query evaluation and a local evaluation depending on the query selectivity, while Huang et al. [2011] use a hybrid approach between MapReduce and evaluation on multiple centralized RDF stores. We view this diver-

Table 4.2: Comparison of query processing strategies (*Continues.*)

System	Query Framework	Query Processing Strategy
SHARD [Rohloff and Schantz, 2011]	MapReduce-based	Left-deep query plans (1 job for each join)
PigSPARQL [Schätzle et al., 2011]	MapReduce-based	Translation of SPARQL queries to PigLatin
HadoopRDF [Husain et al., 2011]	MapReduce-based	Bushy query plans (as many joins as possible in each job)
RAPID+ [Ravindra et al., 2011]	MapReduce-based	Intermediate nested algebra for grouping joins in one job
Zhang et al. [Zhang et al., 2012]	MapReduce-based	Cost-based selection of jobs
MAPSIN [Przyjaciel- Zablocki et al., 2012]	MapReduce-based	Map-side index nested loops
EAGRE [Zhang et al., 2013]	MapReduce-based	Scanning only the data blocks relevant to the query
H₂RDF [Papailiou et al., 2012]	MapReduce-based & local evaluation	Hybrid approach depending on the query selectivity
Rya [Crainiceanu et al., 2012]	Local evaluation	Index nested loops by multiple lookups
AMADA [Aranda-Andújar et al., 2012, Bugiotti et al., 2012, 2014]	Local evaluation	One lookup for each triple pattern and hash join
Stratustore [Stein and Zacharias, 2010a]	Local evaluation	One lookup for each star-join and hashjoin
CumulusRDF [Ladwig and Harth, 2011]	Local evaluation	No join support
Huang et al. [Huang et al., 2011]	Multiple centralized RDF stores & MapReduce-based	Queries processed by the underlying RDF store. If necessary, MapReduce-based join for intermediary results
WARP [Hose and Schenkel, 2013a]	Multiple centralized RDF stores	Queries processed by the underlying RDF store. If necessary, intermediary results are joined at the coordinator

Table 4.2: (*Continued.*) Comparison of query processing strategies

Partout [Galarraga et al., 2012]	Distributed/parallel evaluation	Query plan using merge joins spanning across many nodes
TriaD [Gurajada et al., 2014]	Distributed/parallel evaluation (MPI)	Asynchronous query evaluation with join ahead pruning via graph summarization
Trinity.RDF [Zeng et al., 2013]	Graph-oriented	Traversal of the RDF graph
Spartex [Abdelaziz et al., 2017b]	Graph-oriented	Traversal of the RDF graph
Stylus [He et al., 2017]	Graph-oriented	Partial evaluation & assembly

sity as proof of the current interest in exploring various methods—and their combinations—for massively distributed RDF query processing.

CHAPTER 5

SPARQL Query Optimization for the Cloud

Query optimization has a crucial impact on the performance of SPARQL query evaluation in a massively parallel environment. In particular, query planning determines how a SPARQL query will be decomposed and evaluated across multiple nodes. In this chapter we focus on the concepts and algorithms involved in SPARQL query planning for the cloud. As SPARQL queries are quite join-intensive, i.e., they often comprise many join operations; join evaluation is critical for query performance, thus we will mostly focus on its performance. In a cloud environment, join evaluation is sped up first, thanks to the ability of running each individual join as a parallel MapReduce program (intra-operator parallelism); second, by avoiding data shuffling among the nodes whenever possible (preferring local join evaluation); and third, by intelligently planning the query so that multiple joins can be evaluated in parallel whenever possible (inter-operator parallelism).

Section 5.1 discusses the spaces of logical plans considered in cloud RDF processing systems. As we will see, these spaces depart from the traditional query optimization setting, in particular by considering n-ary joins, for some n higher than 2. We devote Section 5.2 to the presentation of algorithms used to traverse this search space, a challenging task since it is significantly larger than others previously studied.

5.1 QUERY PLAN SEARCH SPACE

A logical query plan represents the steps required for a query to be evaluated, in particular (most significantly) the join ordering. In its most general form, a logical query plan is a rooted directed acyclic graph (DAG) whose nodes are logical operators. As already discussed in the previous chapter, the core operators considered in this setting are:

- triple pattern scan, which reads all the triples (potentially from several storage nodes) matching a certain triple pattern; this operator collapses the traditional scan and select logical operators into one; and

- n-ary join, for some $n \geq 2$, in which several inputs are joined on a set of common variables. Given that each variable corresponds to a triple subject or object (most frequently) or property (less often), the joins serve to "stitch" together partial query answers toward building full BGP answers.

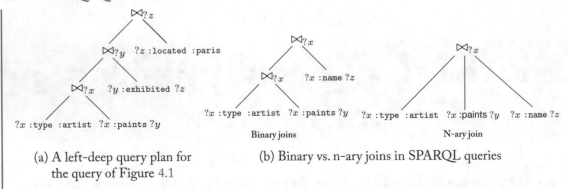

(a) A left-deep query plan for
the query of Figure 4.1

(b) Binary vs. n-ary joins in SPARQL queries

Figure 5.1: SPARQL query plans.

Node lo_i is a parent of node lo_j *iff* the output of lo_i is an input of lo_j. Often, but not always, plans are in fact trees, that is, each node has exactly one parent. Figure 5.1 shows several sample query plans for the query in Figure 4.1.

Query plans can be: (i) linear trees, where one child of each join operator is a leaf; without loss of generality, considering that the non-leaf operator is always the first child of its parent, linear trees can be reduced to left-deep ones; or (ii) bushy trees, where two or more children of an operator can be joins. All the plans in Figure 5.1 are linear. Following a popular heuristic introduced in centralized database management systems, most works on SPARQL query processing only consider left-deep plans, which leads to a significant reduction in the search space. For a query over m triple patterns, there are $m!$ possible linear plans, whereas there are $O(m^3)$ bushy ones. In contrast, some recent systems explore both linear and bushy plans; the main interest of the latter is to exploit the parallel computing potential of a MapReduce environment. Join operators at the same level in a bushy plan can be executed in parallel.

Another dimension that distinguishes the different works is the use of binary joins only vs. n-ary joins for some $n > 2$. SPARQL queries where a variable is shared by more than two triple patterns are quite frequent. In these cases, instead of joining the triple patterns pairwise, one can use an n-way join (with $n > 2$) to join all these triple patterns at the same time. Figure 5.1 illustrates the difference a SPARQL query containing three triple patterns, which have ?x as a common variable. The interest of n-ary join operators is to compute in a single operation the result of joins across more than one relation. Traditional query evaluation algorithms were developed at a time where the available memory was often the bottleneck, and evaluating several join conditions simultaneously (in a single operator) was not an interesting option, since it would have required more memory to hold the necessary data structures. This limitation no longer applies in modern environments, and in particular to parallel join algorithms available in our setting.

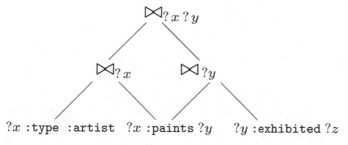

Figure 5.2: Triple pattern (`?x :paints ?y`) is used in two join operators.

Finally, a dimension which impacts the search space is whether a node in the plan (either triple scan or a join operator) can be input to only one, or to several other nodes (typically joins). When each node has at most one parent, the plan is a tree; otherwise, it is DAG. Using the results of a triple pattern or of a join in more than one join operators in a DAG plan is interesting when the reused result is highly selective with respect to its join partners. Figure 5.2 shows an example where triple pattern (`?x :paints ?y`) is used for joining with triple pattern (`?x :type :artist`) on `?x` and with triple pattern (`?y :exhibited ?z`) on variable `?y`. Such a query plan is beneficial when there are only few triple patterns with property `:paints` and thus will decrease the size of both input relations of the final join.

Early works, such as SHARD [Rohloff and Schantz, 2011], use binary left-deep trees to evaluate a SPARQL query. In this case, one MapReduce job is required per triple pattern (as discussed in Section 4.1.2). This leads to $n + 1$ jobs for a query with n triple patterns which leads to poor performance.

To overcome the inefficiency of early works stemming from significant overhead of a MapReduce job [Condie et al., 2010], more recent MapReduce-based proposals use the heuristic of producing query plans that require *the least number of jobs*. Although traditional selectivity-based optimization techniques may decrease the intermediary results, they also lead to a growth in the number of jobs, and thus, to worse query plans with respect to query response time. Therefore, the ultimate goal of such proposals is to produce query plans in the shape of *balanced bushy trees* with the minimum height possible. HadoopRDF [Husain et al., 2011], H₂RDF+ [Papailiou et al., 2013], RAPID+ [Ravindra et al., 2011], and Cliquesquare [Goasdoué et al., 2015] are systems that try to achieve the above goal. A join among two or more triple patterns is performed on the same single variable. Within a job, one or more joins can be performed as long as they are on different variables. When the query has only one join variable, only one job suffices for query evaluation.

In HadoopRDF [Husain et al., 2011] a heuristic is used based where as many joins as possible are performed in each job leading to a query plan with the least number of MapReduce jobs. Figure 5.3 demonstrates a possible query plan produced by HadoopRDF for the example query of Figure 4.1. In the first job, the joins on variables $?x$ and $?z$ are computed between the

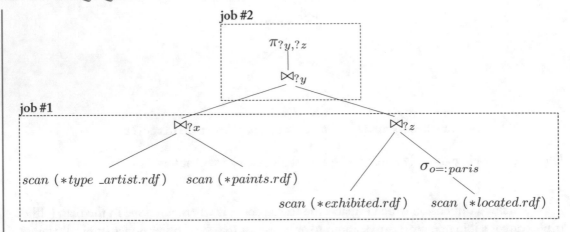

Figure 5.3: Bushy query plan in MapReduce as produced by HadoopRDF based on Husain et al. [2011].

first and the last two triple patterns, respectively. The second job joins the intermediate results of the first job on variable $?y$. The same heuristic is used in H_2RDF+ [Papailiou et al., 2013] for non-selective queries.

A similar approach is followed in RAPID+ [Ravindra et al., 2011] where an intermediate nested algebra is proposed for maximizing the degree of parallelism during join evaluations and reducing MapReduce jobs. This is achieved by interpreting star joins (triple patterns that share the same variable on the subject) as groups of triples and defining new operators on these triple groups. Queries with k star-shaped subqueries are translated into a MapReduce flow with k MapReduce jobs. The proposed algebra is integrated with Pig Latin [Olston et al., 2008].

In Huang et al. [2011] complex queries, which cannot be evaluated completely by the underlying RDF store due to the partitioning scheme, are evaluated within MapReduce for joining the results from different partitions. A query is decomposed in subqueries that can be evaluated independently at every partition, and then the intermediary results are joined through MapReduce jobs sequentially. This creates left-deep query plans with the independent subqueries as leaves. The number of MapReduce jobs increases with the number of subqueries. Figure 5.4 shows how the example query of Figure 4.1 is evaluated based on a partitioned store providing the 1-hop guarantee shown in Figure 3.3. The query is decomposed into two subqueries; the first one contains all three triple patterns, while the second one contains only the last triple pattern. The results from the two subqueries are joined in a MapReduce job.

In Cliquesquare [Goasdoué et al., 2015], each level of a plan is executed as a single MapReduce job. Thus, Cliquesquare aims at producing plans as flat as possible. The optimization algorithm of Cliquesquare is guaranteed to find at least one of the flattest plans (see Chapter 5). These plans contain n-ary star equi-joins at all levels of a plan. In WARP [Hose and Schenkel,

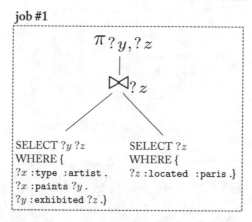

Figure 5.4: Query plan as executed based on Huang et al. [2011].

2013a] and RAPID+ [Ravindra et al., 2011], the authors proposed to use bushy trees with the leaf level allowing for n-ary joins ($n \geq 2$) while the intermediate levels only use binary joins.

5.2   PLANNING ALGORITHMS

After the query plan search space is defined, the query optimizer explores the possible query plans and chooses one to evaluate. Usually the goal is to find a plan that minimizes the query response time (optimal plan). In the database literature there are different algorithms for building and finding the optimal query plan ranging from dynamic programming [Selinger et al., 1979] to randomized algorithms [Ioannidis, 1996]. In our setting, the question is how to *decompose* (i.e., split) the query plan in order to evaluate it in a massively parallel manner and/or in which *order* the triple patterns should be evaluated. Below, Section 5.2.1 focuses on exhaustive approaches, before discussing heuristics-based approaches in Section 5.2.2, dynamic programming approaches in Section 5.2.3, and greedy in Section 5.2.4.

5.2.1   EXHAUSTIVE APPROACHES

Enumerating all plans which only use binary joins is a well-studied problem in the context of centralized relational databases. Enumerating all plans which use n-ary joins is a less-studied problem of much interest in the context of cloud RDF data management.

This first algorithms for that purpose are provided in CliqueSquare [Goasdoué et al., 2015]. The authors represent a SPARQL query as a *variable graph* where each node is a triple pattern, and there is an undirected edge with label v between two nodes *iff* share common variable v. Figure 5.5 shows the variable graphs for two BGP queries.

At the core of CliqueSquare's query optimization approach are the *cliques*. Each clique is a (complete) subgraph of the variable graph, such that all the edges of the clique share the same

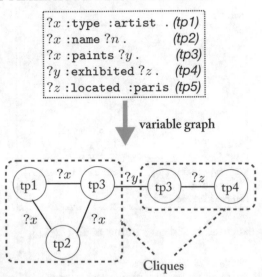

Figure 5.5: A BGP query, its variable graph, and sample cliques as defined in CliqueSquare based on Goasdoué et al. [2015].

label; in other words, a clique corresponds to a set of query triples which share one or several common variables. The blue dotted rectangles in Figure 5.5 show sample cliques in the variable graph. CliqueSquare's plan enumeration algorithm is as follows:

1. Given a query (thus, a variable graph), a *decomposition* of the graph is a set of cliques which cover all the nodes of the variable graph. From the variable graph, a first decomposition is chosen (there are many ways to do so, as we explain below).

2. Each clique from the chosen decomposition which consists of more than one triple pattern is transformed into an *n*-ary join of all its triple patterns. The join result features all the query variables that appeared in one of its inputs.

3. The variable graph is then *reduced* (transformed into another, smaller graph) having:

   • a node for each clique in the decomposition chosen at step 1; and

   • an edge between two nodes, labeled with a variable, whenever these nodes share the respective variable.

4. The above process is repeated from step 1 until the variable graph has exactly one node. At this point, all the query triples have been joined, which corresponds to the root of a query plan.

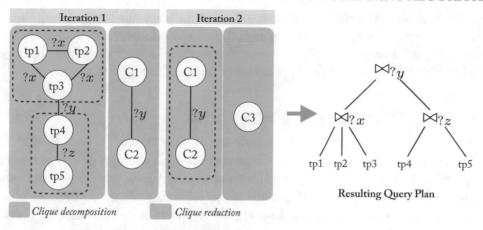

Figure 5.6: CliqueSquare algorithm illustration.

Figure 5.6 illustrates the clique decomposition-reduction steps for the variable graph of Figure 5.5. In the first iteration the clique decomposition outputs two cliques: one for variable ?x and one for variable ?z. In the reduction step of the same iteration, these cliques are reduced to nodes in the graph joined by edge ?y. Clique $C1$ denotes the join of tp_1 with tp_2, while clique C_2 denotes the join of tp_3 with tp_4. In the second iteration, the clique decomposition selects the only clique possible and the clique reduction reduces the graph to one node and, thus, the algorithm terminates. The final node denotes the join between the intermediate results of the two previously identified joins. On the right-hand side, we show the resulted query plan.

It can be easily shown that any logical plan using triple pattern scans and n-ary joins results from a certain set of clique decompositions successively chosen in step 1 above. Moreover, clique decompositions can be classified as follows, according to three orthogonal criteria.

- A decomposition may rely on *maximal* cliques only, or it may consider both *partial* and maximal cliques. A clique is maximal in a variable graph if no triple pattern could be added to it while still respecting the clique definition; partial cliques are those which are not maximal.

- A decomposition may be *partition*, when each triple pattern appears exactly in one clique, or not, i.e., a triple may appear in several cliques.

- A decomposition may be *minimum-size*, meaning that its number of cliques is smallest among all possible decompositions of a given variable graph or not.

The above three orthogonal choices lead to a total of eight search spaces for logical plans based on n-ary joins. Four of them (those where all decompositions are variable graph partitions) comprise tree plans, while the other four lead to DAGs. The above algorithm can generate any of these spaces by making the appropriate decisions along the three dimensions mentioned above. The authors consider the most interesting logical plan space to be the one obtained by using (i) maximal or partial cliques, which (ii) may or may not form a partition of the variable graph, and (iii) forming minimum-size decompositions of the variable graph(s).

5.2.2   HEURISTICS-BASED APPROACHES

In Wu et al. [2017], the authors propose a variation of Cliquesquare [Goasdoué et al., 2015]. While Cliquesquare aims at producing the flattest plan possible and thus utilizes as many n-way joins as possible, in Wu et al. [2017] they also consider binary joins which may not lead to the flattest plan but to the most efficient. For the n-way joins they use the repartition join, while for the second they use broadcast joins [Li et al., 2014]. In addition, Wu et al. [2017] considers decompositions based on the data partitioning, therefore resulting in tree plans instead of DAG-shaped. Specifically, the authors provide a top-down enumeration algorithm for enumerating the decompositions of a variable graph using memorization. The algorithm is guaranteed to generate each decomposition exactly once. They propose two heuristics. The first one checks if the subquery is a local query, i.e., it can be evaluated locally without any data shuffle. If not, the algorithm considers both n-way joins (if possible) as well as all binary broadcast joins. The second heuristic reduces the input join graph (in the case of large SPARQL queries) by finding the triple patterns that can be processed by a local join and combining them into one node in the join graph. Then, the rest of the enumeration is done as previously. As the join graph reduction is an NP-hard problem, they use a greedy weighted set cover algorithm which approximate solves the problem. An interesting aspect of Wu et al. [2017] is that their algorithm automatically determines which heuristic to use for each incoming query.

Another form of heuristics is used in TensorRDF [Virgilio, 2017], which evaluates triple patterns one after the other resulting in left-deep trees. The order in which the triple patterns are evaluated is very crucial for the query response time. This problem is similar to the join ordering problem in relational databases. As this is very hard to solve, many approaches resort to simple heuristics. The authors define *degree of freedom* (DOF) of a triple pattern tp as the difference between the number of variables and the number of constants contained in tp. As such, the DOF can take values from the set $\{+3, +1, -1, -3\}$. For instance, the triple pattern `?x :type :artist` has DOF equal to -1, while the triple pattern `?x :paints ?y` has DOF equal to $+1$. Then, they heuristically evaluate the triple patterns in ascending order of their DOF. The intuition of using the DOF as a heuristic is that a triple pattern with low DOF is more constrained and, thus, will produce less intermediate results. Producing less intermediate results usually leads to better response time. When some triple patterns have the same DOF, the one that has common variables with the largest number of triple patterns is chosen, as it will constrain more triple patterns.

5.2.3 DYNAMIC PROGRAMMING

Dynamic programming was first used in the System R paper [Selinger et al., 1979]. It is a dynamically pruning, exhaustive search algorithm which recursively builds bottom up the query plan by pruning suboptimal subplans. Partout [Galarraga et al., 2012] leverages the dynamic programming query-planning algorithm produced by RDF-3X. Although the initial algorithm proposed was for left-deep binary query plans, there have been several extensions for busy query plans and for n-ary joins [Moerkotte and Neumann, 2006, 2008]. In Papailiou et al. [2015], the authors extend H2RDF+ [Papailiou et al., 2013] with query caching and leverage the DPccp algorithm proposed in Moerkotte and Neumann [2006].

The order in which the triple patterns are evaluated plays a significant role in graph-based systems, similar to with the relational-based ones, as it affects the number of messages that will be sent in the network. In Zeng et al. [2013], the authors propose a cost-based optimization based on dynamic programming and a selectivity estimation technique capturing the correlation between pairs of triples in order to automatically choose a suitable triple pattern evaluation order.

5.2.4 GREEDY APPROACHES

Greedy approaches make the locally optimal choice at each step with the assumption that this choice will lead to the global optimum. Although they may fail to generate the optimal plan, they are inexpensive and, thus, they are used often in query optimizers.

H2RDF+ [Papailiou et al., 2013] follows this approach for creating the query plans on the fly (dynamically during query evaluation). As discussed earlier, H2RDF+ [Papailiou et al., 2013] produces *n*-ary left-deep query plans. Therefore, to build the query plan it is necessary to determine the join ordering. H2RDF+ uses a greedy approach for that. In each step of the query evaluation, it selects the join that incurs the minimum cost based on their cost model.

HadoopRDF [Husain et al., 2011] also follows a greedy approach based on a heuristic. The heuristic first selects the joins that process the largest number of join variables and, thus, leaves the fewest number of variables that need to be joined for the next step. The assumption is that if a large number of join variables is processed together, the query plan will result in the smallest number of MapReduce jobs and, thus, incur less execution cost.

5.3 SUMMARY

Table 5.1 summarizes the different optimization methods of the RDF systems by showing the types of joins they use, the type of query trees they support, and the query planning algorithm they use.

In the experimental study of Abdelaziz et al. [2017a], it is shown that most systems are optimized for specific datasets and query types. For example, among the MapReduce-based systems, the optimization technique of CliqueSquare works well for complex queries where

Table 5.1: Query optimization comparison

System	Join Type	Plan Shape	Planning Algorithm
SHARD [Rohloff and Schantz, 2011]	Binary	Left-deep tree	–
TensorRDF [Virgilio, 2017]	Binary	Left-deep tree	Heuristics
RAPID+ [Ravindra et al., 2011]	n-ary only in leaf-level	Left-deep tree	–
H$_2$RDF [Papailiou et al., 2012]	n-ary	Left-deep tree	Greedy
H$_2$RDF+ [Papailiou et al., 2015]	n-ary	Bushy tree	Dynamic Programming
Partout [Galarraga et al., 2012]	Binary	Left-deep tree	Dynamic Programming
WARP [Hose and Schenkel, 2013a]	n-ary only in leaf-level	Bushy tree	–
HadoopRDF [Husain et al., 2011]	n-ary	Bushy tree	Greedy
CliqueSquare [Goasdoué et al., 2015]	n-ary	Bushy DAG	Clique decomposition
[Wu et al., 2017]	n-ary	Bushy tree	Top-down with heuristics

its flat plans significantly reduce the overhead of distributed joins, while, for selective queries, H$_2$RDF avoids the overhead of MapReduce by executing them locally.

CHAPTER 6

RDFS Reasoning in the Cloud

In Chapter 2, we introduced the core RDF feature called *entailment*, which allows inferring implicit triples that hold within a graph given a set of entailment rules. The role of *inference* (or reasoning) is important in an RDF data management context. Recall that the semantics of an RDF graph is that of its *RDFS closure*, which comprises both its explicit and implicit (i.e., entailed) triples. Generally, there are three methods to handle RDFS entailment:

- *RDFS closure computation*: compute and materialize all entailed triples;

- *query reformulation*: reformulate a given query to take into account entailed triples; and

- *hybrid*: some mix of the two above approaches.

The first method requires computing the entire RDFS closure prior to query processing, while the second (reformulation) is executed at query time. Finally, in the hybrid approach, some entailed data is computed statically and some reformulation is done at query time. An experimental comparison of these RDFS reasoning methods can be found for a centralized setting in Goasdoué et al. [2013] and for a distributed one in Kaoudi and Koubarakis [2013].

We classify the cloud-based systems that support RDFS reasoning according to these three categories. We also consider parallel/distributed approaches that were not necessarily intended for the cloud but can be easily deployed therein. The main challenge faced by these systems is to be complete (answer queries by taking into account both the explicit *and* the implicit triples) even though the data is distributed. At the same time, the total volume of shuffled data should be minimized to not degrade performance.

6.1 REASONING THROUGH RDFS CLOSURE COMPUTATION

One of the most widely spread inference methods for RDF is the precomputation and materialization of all entailed triples, also called *RDFS closure* computation. This method works in a bottom-up fashion; new RDF triples are exhaustively generated based on the RDFS entailment rules and stored until no more new triples can be produced. A query is then evaluated on the RDFS closure and yields a complete answer, taking into account both the given RDF triples and the entailed ones. Although this approach has minimal requirements during query answering, it needs a significant amount of time and space to compute and store all inferred data. For this

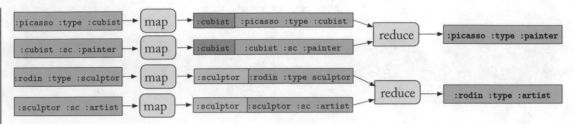

Figure 6.1: MapReduce-based application of rule i_2 of Table 2.2 (page 9).

reason, the parallel processing paradigm of MapReduce is suitable for computing the RDFS closure.

One of the first works providing RDFS closure computation algorithms in a parallel environment is WebPie [Urbani et al., 2009]. RDF data is stored in a distributed file system and the RDFS entailment rules of Table 2.2 are used for precomputing the RDFS closure through MapReduce jobs.

First, observe in Table 2.2 (page 9) that the rules having two triples in the body imply a join between the two triples because they have a common value. See, for example, rule s_1 where the object of the first triple should be the same as the subject of the second one. By selecting the appropriate triple attributes as the output key of the map task, the triples having a common element will meet at the same reducer. Then, at the reducer, the rule can be applied to generate a new triple, thus allowing to parallelize inference. Figure 6.1 illustrates the application of rule i_2 from Table 2.2 within a MapReduce job. In the map phase, the triples are read and a key-value pair is output. The key is the subject or object of the triple, depending on its type, and the value is the triple itself. All the triples generated with the same key meet at the same reducer where the new triple is produced.

Second, entailed triples can also be used as input in the rules. For instance, in the example of Figure 2.2, the entailed triple (:picasso, :type, :painter) can be used to infer the triple (:picasso, :type, :artist). Thus, to compute the RDFS closure, repeated execution of MapReduce jobs is needed until a fixpoint is reached, that is, no new triples are generated.

In WebPie [Urbani et al., 2009, 2012], three optimization techniques are proposed to achieve a fixpoint as soon as possible. The first one starts by the observation that in each RDFS rule with a two-triples body, one of the two is always a schema triple. Since RDF schemas are usually much smaller than RDF datasets, the authors propose to replicate the schema at each node and keep it in memory. Then, each rule can be applied directly either in the map phase or in the reduce phase of a job, given that the schema is available at each node.

The second optimization consists of applying rules in the reduce phase to take advantage of triple grouping and thus avoid redundant data generation. If the rules are applied in the map phase, many redundant triples can be generated. For example, Figure 6.2 shows that for the application of rule i_3, in the map phase, the same triple is produced three times. On the

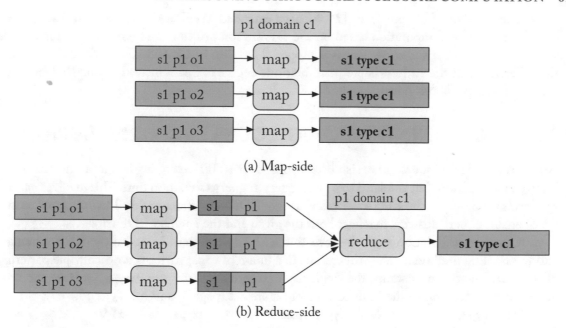

Figure 6.2: Map-side and reduce-side application of rule i_3 of Table 2.2 when schema triples are kept in memory.

other hand, Figure 6.2 demonstrates how rule i_3 can be applied in the reduce phase causing no redundancy.

Finally, in Urbani et al. [2009, 2012] the authors propose an application order for RDFS rules based on their interdependencies so that the required number of MapReduce cycles is minimized. For example, rule i_3 depends on rule i_1; output triples of i_1 are input triples of i_3. Thus, it is more efficient to first apply rule i_1 and then i_3. Thus, the authors show that one can *process each rule only once* and obtain the RDFS closure with the minimum number of MapReduce jobs.

At the same time as Urbani et al. [2009], the authors of Weaver and Hendler [2009] present a similar method for computing the RDFS closure based on the complete set of entailment rules of W3C [2014a] in a parallel way using a message passing interface (MPI). In Weaver and Hendler [2009] they show that the full set of RDFS rules of W3C [2014a] has certain properties that allow for an *embarrassingly parallel* algorithm, meaning that the interdependencies between the rules can easily be handled by ordering them appropriately. This means that the RDFS reasoning task can be divided into completely independent tasks that can be executed in parallel by separate processes. Similarly, with Urbani et al. [2009], each process has access to all schema triples, while data triples are split equally among the processes, and reasoning takes place in parallel.

The authors of Urbani et al. [2009] have extended WebPie in Urbani et al. [2010] to enable the closure computation based on the OWL Horst rules [ter Horst, 2005a]. Finally, a similar proposal with the above works is proposed later on in Cichlid [Gu et al., 2015], with the difference that the authors implement their rule engine in Spark instead of MapReduce and can, thus, achieve better performance.

6.2   REASONING THROUGH QUERY REFORMULATION

An alternative technique that has also been adopted for RDFS reasoning is computing only the inferred information that is related to a given query at query evaluation time. This involves *query reformulation* based on the RDF schema and a set of RDFS entailment rules. Thus, reformulation (also) enables query answers to reflect both the given and the entailed RDF triples.

Query reformulation works by rewriting each triple pattern based on the RDF schema and the RDFS entailment rules. This results in a union of triple patterns for each triple pattern of the initial query. For instance, the single triple pattern query $q =$ (?x, :type, artist) should be rewritten according to the RDF schema of Figure 2.2 (page 7) and rule i_2 as q':

$q' =$ (?x, :type, :artist) $\lor$ (?x, :type, :painter) $\lor$ (?x, :type, :cubist) $\lor$
(?x, :type, :sculptor)

Reformulating large conjunctive queries leads to syntactically large and complex queries, for which many evaluation strategies can be devised. Such a query can be evaluated as a conjunction of unions of triple patterns, with the disadvantage of joining many intermediary results produced by each union query; or, it can be evaluated as a union of conjunctive queries, with the drawback of evaluating repeatedly those fragments which are common across the conjunctive queries. It is important to observe that such common fragments are sure to exist, since each conjunctive query features one atom from the reformulation of each initial query atoms. As a simple example, consider a conjunctive SPARQL query consisting atoms a_1, a_2, and a_3, which are reformulated respectively into the atom sets $\{a_1', a_1''\}$, $\{a_2', a_2'', a_2'''\}$, and $\{a_3', a_3''\}$. This results into $2 \times 3 \times 2 = 12$ conjunctive queries, in other words:

$$q^{ref} = \begin{array}{l} a_1', a_2', a_3' \ \cup \ a_1', a_2'', a_3' \ \cup \ a_1', a_2''', a_3' \ \cup \\ a_1'', a_2', a_3' \ \cup \ a_1'', a_2'', a_3' \ \cup \ a_1'', a_2''', a_3' \ \cup \\ a_1', a_2', a_3'' \ \cup \ a_1', a_2'', a_3'' \ \cup \ a_1', a_2''', a_3'' \ \cup \\ a_1'', a_2', a_3'' \ \cup \ a_1'', a_2'', a_3'' \ \cup \ a_1'', a_2''', a_3'' \end{array}$$

It is easy to identify pairs of conjunctive queries in the above reformulation q^{ref} sharing two atoms, e.g., a_1', a_2', a_3' and a_1'', a_2', a_3', and yet another set of union terms in q^{ref} share one atom. The repeated evaluation of such atoms is one reason why query answering through reformulation may be quite inefficient [Bursztyn et al., 2015b, Goasdoué et al., 2013].

HadoopRDF [Husain et al., 2011] is the only system, among those previously mentioned, that injects some RDFS reasoning within its query processing framework; it is based on the first approach described above. More specifically, query reformulation is implicitly done during the selection of the files that must be scanned in order to start processing the query. For a given triple pattern, instead of scanning only the file that corresponds to the predicate of that pattern, the files corresponding to all the predicates occurring in the *reformulated* triple pattern are scanned, and then the query is processed as described in Chapter 4. This leads to evaluating a conjunction of unions of triple patterns.

The RDFS reasoning process in Husain et al. [2011] is based only on the RDFS *subclass hierarchy*, which means among the rules shown in Figure 2.2, only rules s_1 and i_2 are considered.

6.3   HYBRID TECHNIQUES

Existing proposals from the literature combine the above reasoning approaches, that is, they precompute entailed triples for some part of the RDF data, while reformulation may still be performed at query time.

A common technique in this area is to precompute the RDFS closure of the RDF schema so that query reformulation can be made faster. This works well because the RDF schema is usually very small compared to the data, it seldom changes, and it is always used for the RDFS reasoning process. This approach is followed in Crainiceanu et al. [2012] and Urbani et al. [2011a].

Rya [Crainiceanu et al., 2012] computes the entailed triples of the RDF schema in MapReduce after loading the RDF data into the key-value store, where the RDFS closure is also stored. One MapReduce cycle is used for each level of the subclass hierarchy.

In QueryPie [Urbani et al., 2011a], the authors focus on the parallel evaluation of single triple-pattern queries according to OWL Horst entailment rules [ter Horst, 2005a], which is a superset of the RDFS entailment rules. They build and-or trees where the *or* level is used for the rules and the *and* level is used for the rules' antecedents. The root of the tree is the query triple pattern. To improve performance, entailed schema triples are precomputed so that the and-or tree can be pruned. The system is built on top of Ibis [Bal et al., 2010], a framework which facilitates the development of parallel distributed applications.

Another hybrid approach that is introduced in Kaoudi and Koubarakis [2013] for structured overlay networks and can be deployed in a cloud is the use of the magic-sets-rule rewriting algorithm [Bancilhon et al., 1986]. The basic idea is that, given a query, rules are rewritten using information from the query so that the precomputation of entailed triples generates only the triples required by the query. The benefit of using the new rules in the bottom-up evaluation is that it focuses only on data which is associated with the query and hence no unnecessary information is generated. Such a technique is particularly helpful in application scenarios where knowledge about the query workload is available, and therefore only the triples needed by the workload are precomputed and stored.

Table 6.1: Comparison of reasoning techniques

System	Reasoning Technique	Means for Reasoning	RDFS Fragment	Query Answering
WebPie [Urbani et al., 2009, 2012]	Closure computation	MapReduce	Minimal RDFS	No
Weaver et al. [Weaver and Hendler, 2009]	Closure computation	MPI	Full RDFS	No
WebPie [Urbani et al., 2010]	Closure computation	MapReduce	OWL Horst	No
HadoopRDF [Husain et al., 2011]	Query reformulation	Pellet reasoner to find input files	RDFS subclass only	Conjunctive
Rya [Crainiceanu et al., 2012]	Hybrid	MapReduce	RDFS subclass only	Conjunctive
QueryPie [Urbani et al., 2011a]	Hybrid	Ibis framework	OWL Hors	Single triple patterns

6.4   SUMMARY

Table 6.1 summarizes the works that either focus on RDFS reasoning or provide support for it. The table spells out the reasoning method implemented in each system, the underlying framework on which reasoning takes place, the fragment of entailment rules supported, and the type of queries supported for query answering (if applicable). The works Urbani et al. [2009, 2010], Weaver and Hendler [2009], which focus on RDFS closure computation, do not consider query answering; one could deploy in conjunction with any of them any of the query processing algorithms presented in Chapter 4.

CHAPTER 7

Concluding Remarks

RDF has been successfully used to encode heterogeneous semi-structured data in a variety of application contexts. Efficiently processing large volumes of RDF data defeats the possibilities of a single centralized system. In this context, recent research has sought to take advantage of the large-scale parallelization possibilities provided by the cloud while also enjoying features such as automatic scale-up and scale-down of resource allocation as well as some level of resilience to system failures.

In this book we have studied the state of the art in RDF data management in a cloud environment as well as the most recent advances of RDF data management in parallel/distributed architectures that were not necessarily intended for the cloud, but can easily be deployed therein. We described existing systems and proposals which can handle large volumes of RDF data by classifying them along different dimensions and highlighting their benefits and limitations. The four dimensions we investigated are data storage, query processing, query optimization, and reasoning. These are the fundamental aspects one should first consider when handling RDF data. There are other aspects of RDF data management, such as data profiling [Kruse et al., 2016] and statistical learning [Nickel et al., 2016], which we did not focus on in this book.

Overall, we observed a great density of systems using MapReduce-style frameworks and DFS, as well as key-value systems with local clients for performing more complex tasks, presumably because such underlying infrastructures are very easy to use. Among all possibilities for building an RDF store, each option has its trade-offs. For instance, key-value stores offer a fine-granular indexing mechanism allowing very fast triple pattern matching; however, they do not rival the parallelism offered by MapReduce-style frameworks for processing efficiently queries, and, thus, most systems perform joins locally at a single site. Although this approach may be efficient for very selective queries with few intermediate results, it is not scalable for analytical-style queries which need to access big portions of RDF data. For the latter, a MapReduce-style framework is more appropriate, especially if a fully parallel query plan is employed. Approaches based on centralized RDF stores are well suited for star-join queries, since triples sharing the same subject are typically grouped on the same site. Thus, the centralized RDF engine available on that site can be leveraged to process efficiently the query for the respective data subset; overall, such queries are efficiently evaluated by the set of single-site engines working in parallel. In contrast, path queries which need to traverse the subsets of the RDF graph stored at distinct sites involve more communications between machines and thus their evaluation is less efficient. Finally, it may be worth noting that a parallel processor built out of a set of single-site ones leaves open issues such as fault tolerance and load balancing, issues which are implicitly handled by frameworks such as MapReduce. Considering the variety of requirements (point queries vs. large analytical ones, star vs. chain queries, updates, etc.), a combination of techniques, perhaps with some adaptive flavor taking into account the characteristics of a particular RDF data set and workload, is likely to lead to the best performance overall.

We currently find numerous open problems as the research area of parallel RDF data management has only been around for a few years. RDFS reasoning is an essential functionality of the RDF data model and it needs to be taken into account for RDF stores to provide correct and complete query answers. While some works investigated the parallelization of the RDFS closure computation, the area of query reformulation is so far unexplored in a parallel environment for conjunctive RDF queries. Query reformulation can benefit from techniques for multi-query optimization like the ones proposed in Elghandour and Aboulnaga [2012], Wang and Chan [2013], and scan sharing [Kim et al., 2012], but adapting such techniques for RDF data is not straightforward.

More recently we noticed a great amount of work studying optimization techniques such as query decomposition and join ordering. Query optimization is vital to achieve great system performance. Still, these works are still in their infancy and most of them neglect the RDFS reasoning aspect that may happen during query processing and, thus, affect the optimization algorithm.

In addition, current works focus only on the conjunctive fragment of SPARQL. Although this is the first step toward RDF query processing, SPARQL allows for much more expressive queries, e.g., queries including optional clauses, aggregations, and property paths.[1] New frameworks for RDF style analytics have appeared [Colazzo et al., 2014], which may naturally be adapted to a large-scale (cloud) context. Evaluating such queries in a parallel environment is still an open issue.

---

[1]http://www.w3.org/TR/sparql11-property-paths/

Bibliography

D. J. Abadi, A. Marcus, S. Madden, and K. J. Hollenbach. Scalable semantic web data management using vertical partitioning. In C. Koch, J. Gehrke, M. N. Garofalakis, D. Srivastava, K. Aberer, A. Deshpande, D. Florescu, C. Y. Chan, V. Ganti, C. Kanne, W. Klas, and E. J. Neuhold, Eds., *Proc. of the 33rd International Conference on Very Large Data Bases*, pp. 411–422, ACM, University of Vienna, Austria, September 23–27, 2007. http://www.vldb.org/conf/2007/papers/research/p411-abadi.pdf 26, 37

D. J. Abadi, A. Marcus, S. Madden, and K. Hollenbach. SW-Store: A vertically partitioned DBMS for semantic web data management. *VLDB Journal*, 18(2):385–406, 2009. DOI: 10.1007/s00778-008-0125-y 2

I. Abdelaziz, R. Harbi, S. Salihoglu, P. Kalnis, and N. Mamoulis. Spartex: A vertex-centric framework for RDF data analytics. *PVLDB*, 8(12):1880–1891, 2015. http://www.vldb.org/pvldb/vol8/p1880-abdelaziz.pdf DOI: 10.14778/2824032.2824091 51

I. Abdelaziz, R. Harbi, Z. Khayyat, and P. Kalnis. A survey and experimental comparison of distributed SPARQL engines for very large RDF data. *PVLDB*, 10(13):2049–2060, 2017a. http://www.vldb.org/pvldb/vol10/p2049-abdelaziz.pdf DOI: 10.14778/3151106.3151109 42, 54, 55, 65

I. Abdelaziz, R. Harbi, S. Salihoglu, and P. Kalnis. Combining vertex-centric graph processing with SPARQL for large-scale RDF data analytics. *IEEE Transactions on Parallel and Distributed Systems*, 28(12):3374–3388, December 2017b. DOI: 10.1109/tpds.2017.2720174 51, 52

S. Abiteboul, R. Hull, and V. Vianu. *Foundations of Databases*. Addison-Wesley, 1995. http://www-cse.ucsd.edu/users/vianu/book.html 5

S. Abiteboul, I. Manolescu, N. Polyzotis, N. Preda, and C. Sun. XML processing in DHT networks. In G. Alonso, J. A. Blakeley, and A. L. P. Chen, Eds., *Proc. of the 24th International Conference on Data Engineering, ICDE*, pp. 606–615, IEEE, Cancún, México, April 7–12, 2008. DOI: 10.1109/ICDE.2008.4497469 31

A. Abouzeid, K. Bajda-Pawlikowski, D. J. Abadi, A. Rasin, and A. Silberschatz. HadoopDB: An architectural hybrid of MapReduce and DBMS technologies for analytical workloads. *PVLDB*, 2(1):922–933, 2009. http://www.vldb.org/pvldb/2/vldb09-861.pdf DOI: 10.14778/1687627.1687731 37

Accumulo. Apache Accumulo. `http://accumulo.apache.org/`, 2008. 14, 30

P. Adjiman, F. Goasdoué, and M. Rousset. SomeRDFSin the semantic web. *Journal of Data Semantics*, 8:158–181, 2007. DOI: 10.1007/978-3-540-70664-9_6 12

S. Alexaki, V. Christophides, G. Karvounarakis, D. Plexousakis, K. Tolle, B. Amann, I. Fundulaki, M. Scholl, and A. Vercoustre. Managing RDF metadata for community webs. In S. W. Liddle, H. C. Mayr, and B. Thalheim, Eds., *Conceptual Modeling for E-Business and the Web, ER Workshops on Conceptual Modeling Approaches for E-Business and the World Wide Web and Conceptual Modeling*, Salt Lake City, UT, October 9–12, 2000, Proceedings, volume 1921 of *Lecture Notes in Computer Science*, pp. 140–151, Springer, 2000. DOI: 10.1007/3-540-45394-6_13 38

S. Alexaki, V. Christophides, G. Karvounarakis, D. Plexousakis, and K. Tolle. The ICS-FORTH RDFSuite: Managing umi(u):s RDF description bases. In *SemWeb*, 2001. `http://CEUR-WS.org/Vol-40/alexakietal.pdf` 38

A. Alexandrov, R. Bergmann, S. Ewen, J. Freytag, F. Hueske, A. Heise, O. Kao, M. Leich, U. Leser, V. Markl, F. Naumann, M. Peters, A. Rheinländer, M. J. Sax, S. Schelter, M. Höger, K. Tzoumas, and D. Warneke. The stratosphere platform for big data analytics. *VLDB Journal*, 23(6):939–964, 2014. DOI: 10.1007/s00778-014-0357-y 18

Amazon Web Services. Amazon Web Services. `http://aws.amazon.com/` 30

A. Aranda-Andújar, F. Bugiotti, J. Camacho-Rodríguez, D. Colazzo, F. Goasdoué, Z. Kaoudi, and I. Manolescu. AMADA: Web data repositories in the Amazon cloud. In X. Chen, G. Lebanon, H. Wang, and M. J. Zaki, Eds., *21st ACM International Conference on Information and Knowledge Management, CIKM'12*, pp. 2749–2751, ACM, Maui, HI, October 29–November 02, 2012. DOI: 10.1145/2396761.2398749 30, 31, 39, 40, 45, 50, 54, 55

M. Arias, J. Fernández, M. Martínez-Prieto, and P. de la Fuente. An empirical study of real-world SPARQL queries. In *1st International Workshop on Usage Analysis and the Web of Data (USEWOD2011)*, 2011. 44

S. Auer, C. Bizer, G. Kobilarov, J. Lehmann, R. Cyganiak, and Z. G. Ives. DBpedia: A nucleus for a Web of open data. In *ISWC*, 2007. DOI: 10.1007/978-3-540-76298-0_52 2

H. E. Bal, J. Maassen, R. V. van Nieuwpoort, N. Drost, R. Kemp, N. Palmer, G. Wrzesinska, T. Kielmann, F. Seinstra, and C. Jacobs. Real-world distributed computing with ibis. *IEEE Computer*, 43(8):54–62, 2010. DOI: 10.1109/mc.2010.184 71

F. Bancilhon, D. Maier, Y. Sagiv, and J. D. Ullman. Magic sets and other strange ways to implement logic programs (extended abstract). In *PODS*, 1986. DOI: 10.1145/6012.15399 71

D. Battré, S. Ewen, F. Hueske, O. Kao, V. Markl, and D. Warneke. Nephele/PACTs: A programming model and execution framework for web-scale analytical processing. In *Proc. of the 1st ACM Symposium on Cloud Computing, SoCC*, pp. 119–130, Indianapolis, IN, June 10-11, 2010. DOI: 10.1145/1807128.1807148 18

D. J. Beckett. The design and implementation of the Redland RDF application framework. In V. Y. Shen, N. Saito, M. R. Lyu, and M. E. Zurko, Eds., *Proc. of the 10th International World Wide Web Conference, WWW 10*, pp. 449–456, ACM, Hong Kong, China, May 1–5, 2001. DOI: 10.1145/371920.372099. 38

T. Berners-Lee. Linked data—design issues. `http://www.w3.org/DesignIssues/LinkedD ata.html`, 2006. 1

T. Berners-Lee, J. Hendler, and O. Lassila. The semantic web. *Scientific American*, 284(5):34–43, May 2001. DOI: 10.1038/scientificamerican0501-34 1

S. Blanas, J. M. Patel, V. Ercegovac, J. Rao, E. J. Shekita, and Y. Tian. A comparison of join algorithms for log processing in MapReduce. In *SIGMOD*, 2010. DOI: 10.1145/1807167.1807273 49

M. A. Bornea, J. Dolby, A. Kementsietsidis, K. Srinivas, P. Dantressangle, O. Udrea, and B. Bhattacharjcc. Building an efficient RDF store over a relational database. In *SIGMOD*, pp. 121–132, 2013. DOI: 10.1145/2463676.2463718 2

J. Broekstra and A. Kampman. Sesame: A generic architecture for storing and querying RDF and RDF schema. In *ISWC*, 2002. DOI: 10.1002/0470858060.ch5 2

J. Broekstra, A. Kampman, and F. van Harmelen. Sesame: A generic architecture for storing and querying RDF and RDF schema. In I. Horrocks and J. A. Hendler, Eds., *The Semantic Web—ISWC, 1st International Semantic Web Conference, Proceedings*, Sardinia, Italy, June 9–12, 2002, volume 2342 of *Lecture Notes in Computer Science*, pp. 54–68, Springer, 2002. DOI: 10.1007/3-540-48005-6_7 38

F. Bugiotti, F. Goasdoué, Z. Kaoudi, and I. Manolescu. RDF data management in the Amazon cloud. In D. Srivastava and I. Ari, Eds., *Proc. of the Joint EDBT/ICDT Workshops*, pp. 61–72, ACM, Berlin, Germany, March 30, 2012. DOI: 10.1145/2320765.2320790 39, 40, 45, 54, 55

F. Bugiotti, J. Camacho-Rodríguez, F. Goasdoué, Z. Kaoudi, I. Manolescu, and S. Zampetakis. SPARQL query processing in the cloud. In A. Harth, K. Hose, and R. Schenkel, Eds., *Linked Data Management*, pp. 165–192, Chapman and Hall/CRC, 2014. `http://www.crcnetba se.com/doi/abs/10.1201/b16859-11` 39, 40, 45, 54, 55

D. Bursztyn, F. Goasdoué, and I. Manolescu. Efficient query answering in DL-lite through FOL reformulation (extended abstract). In *Proc. of the 28th International Workshop on Description Logics*, Athens, Greece, June 7–10, 2015a. http://ceur-ws.org/Vol-1350/paper-15.pdf 12

D. Bursztyn, F. Goasdoué, and I. Manolescu. Optimizing reformulation-based query answering in RDF. In G. Alonso, F. Geerts, L. Popa, P. Barceló, J. Teubner, M. Ugarte, J. V. den Bussche, and J. Paredaens, Eds., *Proc. of the 18th International Conference on Extending Database Technology, EDBT*, pp. 265–276, Brussels, Belgium, March 23–27, OpenProceedings.org, 2015b. DOI: 10.5441/002/edbt.2015.24 12, 70

M. Cai and M. R. Frank. RDFPeers: A scalable distributed RDF repository based on a structured peer-to-peer network. In S. I. Feldman, M. Uretsky, M. Najork, and C. E. Wills, Eds., *Proc. of the 13th International Conference on World Wide Web, WWW*, pp. 650–657, ACM, New York, May 17–20, 2004. DOI: 10.1145/988672.988760 26

D. Calvanese, G. De Giacomo, D. Lembo, M. Lenzerini, and R. Rosati. Tractable reasoning and efficient query answering in description logics: The *DL-Lite* family. *Journal of Automated Reasoning*, 39(3):385–429, 2007. DOI: 10.1007/s10817-007-9078-x 12

Cassandra. Apache Cassandra. http://cassandra.apache.org/, 2008. 14, 30

F. Chang, J. Dean, S. Ghemawat, W. C. Hsieh, D. A. Wallach, M. Burrows, T. Chandra, A. Fikes, and R. Gruber. Bigtable: A distributed storage system for structured data. In B. N. Bershad and J. C. Mogul, Eds., *7th Symposium on Operating Systems Design and Implementation (OSDI'06)*, pp. 205–218, USENIX Association, November 6–8, Seattle, WA, 2006. http://www.usenix.org/events/osdi06/tech/chang.html DOI: 10.1145/1365815.1365816 14

E. I. Chong, S. Das, G. Eadon, and J. Srinivasan. An efficient SQL-based RDF querying scheme. In *VLDB*, 2005. 2

D. Colazzo, F. Goasdoué, I. Manolescu, and A. Roatiş. RDF analytics: Lenses over semantic graphs. In *WWW*, 2014. DOI: 10.1145/2566486.2567982 74

T. Condie, N. Conway, P. Alvaro, and J. M. Hellerstein. MapReduce online. In *NSDI*, 2010. 59

A. Crainiceanu, R. Punnoose, and D. Rapp. Rya: A scalable RDF triple store for the clouds. In *Cloud-I Workshop*, 2012. DOI: 10.1145/2347673.2347677 50, 52, 71, 72

G. De Giacomo, D. Lembo, M. Lenzerini, A. Poggi, R. Rosati, M. Ruzzi, and D. F. Savo. MASTRO: A reasoner for effective ontology-based data access. In *Proc. of the 1st International Workshop on OWL Reasoner Evaluation (ORE-2012)*, Manchester, UK, July 1, 2012. http://ceur-ws.org/Vol-858/ore2012_paper7.pdf 12

J. Dean and S. Ghemawat. MapReduce: Simplified data processing on large clusters. In E. A. Brewer and P. Chen, Eds., *6th Symposium on Operating System Design and Implementation (OSDI)*, pp. 137–150, USENIX Association, San Francisco, CA, December 6–8, 2004. `http://www.usenix.org/events/osdi04/tech/dean.html` DOI: 10.1145/1327452.1327492 2, 17

G. DeCandia, D. Hastorun, M. Jampani, G. Kakulapati, A. Lakshman, A. Pilchin, S. Sivasubramanian, P. Vosshall, and W. Vogels. Dynamo: Amazon's highly available key-value store. In T. C. Bressoud and M. F. Kaashoek, Eds., *Proc. of the 21st ACM Symposium on Operating Systems Principles, SOSP*, pp. 205–220, ACM, Stevenson, WA, October 14–17, 2007. DOI: 10.1145/1294261.1294281 17

O. Deshpande, D. S. Lamba, M. Tourn, S. Das, S. Subramaniam, A. Rajaraman, V. Harinarayan, and A. Doan. Building, maintaining, and using knowledge bases: A report from the trenches. In *Proc. of the ACM SIGMOD International Conference on Management of Data*, pp. 1209–1220, 2013. DOI: 10.1145/2463676.2465297 2

J. Dittrich, J. Quiané-Ruiz, A. Jindal, Y. Kargin, V. Setty, and J. Schad. Hadoop++: Making a yellow elephant run like a cheetah (without it even noticing). *PVLDB*, 3(1):518–529, 2010. `http://www.comp.nus.edu.sg/vldb2010/proceedings/files/papers/R46.pdf` DOI: 10.14778/1920841.1920908 14

J. Dittrich, J. Quiané-Ruiz, S. Richter, S. Schuh, A. Jindal, and J. Schad. Only aggressive elephants are fast elephants. *PVLDB*, 5(11):1591–1602, 2012. `http://vldb.org/pvldb/vol5/p1591_jensdittrich_vldb2012.pdf` DOI: 10.14778/2350229.2350272 14

X. L. Dong. Challenges and innovations in building a product knowledge graph. In *Proc. of the 24th ACM SIGKDD International Conference on Knowledge Discovery (keynote), KDD '18*, pp. 2869–2869, 2018. DOI: 10.1145/3219819.3219938 2

Dynamo. Amazon DynamoDB. `http://aws.amazon.com/dynamodb/`, 2012. 14, 30, 39

I. Elghandour and A. Aboulnaga. ReStore: Reusing results of MapReduce jobs. *PVLDB*, 5(6):586–597, 2012. DOI: 10.1145/2213836.2213937 74

O. Erling and I. Mikhailov. RDF support in the virtuoso DBMS. *Networked Knowledge—Networked Media*, pp. 7–24, 2009. DOI: 10.1007/978-3-642-02184-8_2 2

W. Fan, X. Wang, and Y. Wu. Performance guarantees for distributed reachability queries. *PVLDB*, 5(11):1304–1315, 2012. `http://vldb.org/pvldb/vol5/p1304_wenfeifan_vldb2012.pdf` DOI: 10.14778/2350229.2350248 53

L. Galarraga, K. Hose, and R. Schenkel. Partout: A distributed engine for efficient RDF processing. *CoRR*, abs/1212.5636, 2012. `http://arxiv.org/abs/1212.5636` DOI: 10.1145/2567948.2577302 34, 37, 40, 42, 47, 51, 54, 55, 65, 66

Y. Gao, J. Liang, B. Han, M. Yakout, and A. Mohamed. Building a large-scale, accurate and fresh knowledge graph. In *KDD Tutorial*, 2018. 2

S. Ghemawat, H. Gobioff, and S. Leung. The Google file system. In *Proc. of the 19th ACM Symposium on Operating Systems Principles, SOSP*, pp. 29–43, Bolton Landing, NY, October 19–22, 2003. DOI: 10.1145/945445.945450 13

F. Goasdoué, K. Karanasos, J. Leblay, and I. Manolescu. View selection in semantic web databases. *PVLDB*, 5(2):97–108, 2011. `http://www.vldb.org/pvldb/vol5/p097_fran coisgoasdoue_vldb2012.pdf` DOI: 10.14778/2078324.2078326 12

F. Goasdoué, I. Manolescu, and A. Roatiş. Efficient query answering against dynamic RDF databases. In *EDBT*, 2013. DOI: 10.1145/2452376.2452412 67, 70

F. Goasdoué, I. Manolescu, and A. Roatis. Efficient query answering against dynamic RDF databases. In G. Guerrini and N. W. Paton, Eds., *Joint EDBT/ICDT Conferences, EDBT'13 Proceedings*, pp. 299–310, ACM, Genoa, Italy, March 18–22, 2013. DOI: 10.1145/2452376.2452412 12

F. Goasdoué, Z. Kaoudi, I. Manolescu, J. Quiané-Ruiz, and S. Zampetakis. CliqueSquare: Flat plans for massively parallel RDF queries. In J. Gehrke, W. Lehner, K. Shim, S. K. Cha, and G. M. Lohman, Eds., *31st IEEE International Conference on Data Engineering, ICDE*, pp. 771–782, Seoul, South Korea, April 13–17, 2015. DOI: 10.1109/ICDE.2015.7113332 18, 26, 40, 44, 45, 59, 60, 61, 62, 64, 66

G. Gottlob, G. Orsi, and A. Pieris. Ontological queries: Rewriting and optimization. In *Proc. of the 27th International Conference on Data Engineering, ICDE*, pp. 2–13, Hannover, Germany, April 11–16, 2011. DOI: 10.1109/ICDE.2011.5767965 12

R. Gu, S. Wang, F. Wang, C. Yuan, and Y. Huang. Cichlid: Efficient large scale RDFS/OWL reasoning with Spark. In *IEEE International Parallel and Distributed Processing Symposium, IPDPS*, pp. 700–709, Hyderabad, India, May 25–29, 2015. DOI: 10.1109/IPDPS.2015.14 70

S. Gurajada, S. Seufert, I. Miliaraki, and M. Theobald. TriAD: A distributed shared-nothing RDF engine based on asynchronous message passing. In C. E. Dyreson, F. Li, and M. T. Özsu, Eds., *International Conference on Management of Data, SIGMOD*, pp. 289–300, ACM, Snowbird, UT, June 22–27, 2014. DOI: 10.1145/2588555.2610511 38, 40, 47, 51, 54, 55

Hadoop. Apache Hadoop. `http://hadoop.apache.org/`, 2011. 13, 18

M. Hammoud, D. A. Rabbou, R. Nouri, S. Beheshti, and S. Sakr. DREAM: Distributed RDF engine with adaptive query planner and minimal communication. *PVLDB*, 8(6):654–665, 2015. `http://www.vldb.org/pvldb/vol8/p654-Hammoud.pdf` DOI: 10.14778/2735703.2735705 37, 40

S. Harris, N. Lamb, and N. Shadbolt. 4store: The design and implementation of a clustered RDF store. In *In 5th International Workshop on Scalable Semantic Web Knowledge Base Systems (SSWS2009)*, pp. 94–109, 2009. 2

HBase. Apache HBase. http://hbase.apache.org/, 2008. 14, 30

L. He, B. Shao, Y. Li, H. Xia, Y. Xiao, E. Chen, and L. J. Chen. Stylus: A strongly-typed store for serving massive RDF data. *PVLDB*, 11(2):203–216, 2017. DOI: 10.14778/3149193.3149200 33, 40, 52, 53, 54, 55

K. Hose and R. Schenkel. WARP: Workload-aware replication and partitioning for RDF. In C. Y. Chan, J. Lu, K. Nørvåg, and E. Tanin, Eds., *Workshops Proceedings of the 29th IEEE International Conference on Data Engineering, ICDE*, pp. 1–6, Computer Society, Brisbane, Australia, April 8–12, 2013a. DOI: 10.1109/ICDEW.2013.6547414 34, 37, 40, 42, 54, 55, 60, 66

K. Hose and R. Schenkel. WARP: Workload-aware replication and partitioning for RDF. In *DESWEB*, 2013b. DOI: 10.1109/icdew.2013.6547414 47, 51

J. Huang, D. J. Abadi, and K. Ren. Scalable SPARQL querying of large RDF graphs. *PVLDB*, 4(11):1123–1134, 2011. http://www.vldb.org/pvldb/vol4/p1123-huang.pdf 18, 34, 35, 36, 37, 40, 47, 53, 54, 55, 60, 61

M. F. Husain, J. P. McGlothlin, M. M. Masud, L. R. Khan, and B. M. Thuraisingham. Heuristics-based query processing for large RDF graphs using cloud computing. *IEEE Transactions on Knowledge and Data Engineering*, 23(9):1312–1327, 2011. DOI: 10.1109/TKDE.2011.103 18, 26, 40, 44, 45, 54, 55, 59, 60, 65, 66, 70, 71, 72

Y. E. Ioannidis. Query optimization. *ACM Computing Surveys*, 28(1):121–123, March 1996. DOI: 10.1145/234313.234367 61

Z. Kaoudi and M. Koubarakis. Distributed RDFS reasoning over structured overlay networks. *Journal on Data Semantics*, 2013. DOI: 10.1007/s13740-013-0018-0 2, 67, 71

Z. Kaoudi and I. Manolescu. RDF in the clouds: A survey. *VLDB Journal*, 24(1):67–91, 2015. DOI: 10.1007/s00778-014-0364-z 18

Z. Kaoudi, I. Miliaraki, and M. Koubarakis. RDFS reasoning and query answering on top of DHTs. In A. P. Sheth, S. Staab, M. Dean, M. Paolucci, D. Maynard, T. W. Finin, and K. Thirunarayan, Eds., *The Semantic Web—ISWC, 7th International Semantic Web Conference, ISWC*, Karlsruhe, Germany, October 26–30, Proceedings, volume 5318 of *Lecture Notes in Computer Science*, pp. 499–516, Springer, 2008. DOI: 10.1007/978-3-540-88564-1_32 12

Z. Kaoudi, K. Kyzirakos, and M. Koubarakis. SPARQL query optimization on top of DHTs. In P. F. Patel-Schneider, Y. Pan, P. Hitzler, P. Mika, L. Zhang, J. Z. Pan, I. Horrocks, and B. Glimm, Eds., *The Semantic Web—ISWC—9th International Semantic Web Conference, ISWC*, Shanghai, China, November 7–11, Revised Selected Papers, Part I, volume 6496 of *Lecture Notes in Computer Science*, pp. 418–435, Springer, 2010. DOI: 10.1007/978-3-642-17746-0_27 2

G. Karypis and V. Kumar. A fast and high quality multilevel scheme for partitioning irregular graphs. *SIAM Journal on Scientific Computing*, 20(1):359–392, 1998. DOI: 10.1137/s1064827595287997 24, 34, 38

H. Kim, P. Ravindra, and K. Anyanwu. From SPARQL to MapReduce: The journey using a nested triplegroup algebra. *PVLDB*, 4(12):1426–1429, 2011. http://www.vldb.org/pvldb/vol4/p1426-kim.pdf 18, 40

H. Kim, P. Ravindra, and K. Anyanwu. Scan-sharing for optimizing RDF graph pattern matching on MapReduce. In *IEEE Conference on Cloud Computing*, 2012. DOI: 10.1109/cloud.2012.14 74

A. Kiryakov, B. Bishoa, D. Ognyanoff, I. Peikov, Z. Tashev, and R. Velkov. The features of BigOWLIM that enabled the BBC's world cup website. In *Workshop on Semantic Data Management*, 2010. 2

M. König, M. Leclère, M. Mugnier, and M. Thomazo. Sound, complete and minimal UCQ-rewriting for existential rules. *Semantic Web*, 6(5):451–475, 2015. DOI: 10.3233/SW-140153 12

S. Kruse, A. Jentzsch, T. Papenbrock, Z. Kaoudi, J. Quiané-Ruiz, and F. Naumann. RDFind: Scalable conditional inclusion dependency discovery in RDF datasets. In *SIGMOD*, pp. 953–967, 2016. DOI: 10.1145/2882903.2915206 73

G. Ladwig and A. Harth. CumulusRDF: Linked data management on nested key-value stores. In *The 7th International Workshop on Scalable Semantic Web Knowledge Base Systems (SSWS)*, p. 30, 2011. 30, 31, 40, 48, 54, 55

J. K. Lawder and P. J. H. King. Using space-filling curves for multi-dimensional indexing. In B. Lings and K. G. Jeffery, Eds., *Advances in Databases, 17th British National Conference on Databases, BNCOD 17*, Exeter, UK, July 3–5, Proceedings, volume 1832 of *Lecture Notes in Computer Science*, pp. 20–35, Springer, 2000. DOI: 10.1007/3-540-45033-5_3 28

K. Lee and L. Liu. Scaling queries over big RDF graphs with semantic hash partitioning. *PVLDB*, 6(14):1894–1905, 2013. http://www.vldb.org/pvldb/vol6/p1894-lee.pdf DOI: 10.14778/2556549.2556571 18, 34, 36, 40, 42

F. Li, B. C. Ooi, M. T. Özsu, and S. Wu. Distributed data management using MapReduce. *ACM Computing Surveys*, 46(3):31, 2014. DOI: 10.1145/2503009 18, 50, 64

LOD. State of the LOD cloud. `http://www4.wiwiss.fu-berlin.de/lodcloud/state/`, 2011. 2

G. Malewicz, M. H. Austern, A. J. Bik, J. C. Dehnert, I. Horn, N. Leiser, and G. Czajkowski. Pregel: A System for large-scale graph processing. In *Proc. of the 28th ACM Symposium on Principles of Distributed Computing, PODC'09*, p. 6, New York, 2009. DOI: 10.1145/1582716.1582723 51

B. McBride. Jena: A semantic web toolkit. *IEEE Internet Computing*, 6(6):55–59, 2002. `http://doi.ieeecomputersociety.org/10.1109/MIC.2002.1067737` 38

J. McCarthy. Recursive functions of symbolic expressions and their computation by machine, part I. *Communications of the ACM*, 3(4):184–195, 1960. DOI: 10.1145/367177.367199 17

G. Moerkotte and T. Neumann. Analysis of two existing and one new dynamic programming algorithm for the generation of optimal bushy join trees without cross products. In *Proc. of the 32nd International Conference on Very Large Data Bases, VLDB'06*, pp. 930–941, VLDB Endowment, 2006. `http://dl.acm.org/citation.cfm?id=1182635.1164207` DOI: 10.5555/1182635.1164207 65

G. Moerkotte and T. Neumann. Dynamic programming strikes back. In *SIGMOD*, pp. 539–552, 2008. DOI: 10.1145/1376616.1376672 65

S. Muñoz, J. Pérez, and C. Gutierrez. Simple and efficient minimal RDFS. *Web Semantic*, 7(3):220–234, September 2009. DOI: 10.1016/j.websem.2009.07.003 9

T. Neumann and G. Moerkotte. Characteristic sets: Accurate cardinality estimation for RDF queries with multiple joins. In *Proc. of the 27th International Conference on Data Engineering, ICDE*, pp. 984–994, IEEE Computer Society, Hannover, Germany, April 11–16, 2011. DOI: 10.1109/ICDE.2011.5767868 33

T. Neumann and G. Weikum. The RDF-3X engine for scalable management of RDF data. *VLDBJ*, 19(1), 2010a. DOI: 10.1007/s00778-009-0165-y 29, 36, 47

T. Neumann and G. Weikum. The RDF-3X engine for scalable management of RDF data. *VLDBJ*, 19(1), 2010b. DOI: 10.1007/s00778-009-0165-y 2

M. Nickel, K. Murphy, V. Tresp, and E. Gabrilovich. A review of relational machine learning for knowledge graphs. *Proc. of the IEEE*, 104(1):11–33, 2016. DOI: 10.1109/jproc.2015.2483592 73

C. Olston, B. Reed, U. Srivastava, R. Kumar, and A. Tomkins. Pig Latin: A not-so-foreign language for data processing. In *Proc. of the ACM SIGMOD International Conference on Management of Data, SIGMOD*, pp. 1099–1110, Vancouver, BC, Canada, June 10–12, 2008. DOI: 10.1145/1376616.1376726 48, 60

A. Owens, A. Seaborne, and N. Gibbins. Clustered TDB: A clustered triple store for Jena, 2008. http://eprints.ecs.soton.ac.uk/16974/ 2

N. Papailiou, I. Konstantinou, D. Tsoumakos, and N. Koziris. H2RDF: Adaptive query processing on RDF data in the cloud. In A. Mille, F. L. Gandon, J. Misselis, M. Rabinovich, and S. Staab, Eds., *Proc. of the 21st World Wide Web Conference, WWW*, pp. 397–400, ACM, Lyon, France, April 16–20, 2012 (Companion Volume), 2012. DOI: 10.1145/2187980.2188058 18, 29, 30, 31, 40, 52, 54, 55, 66

N. Papailiou, I. Konstantinou, D. Tsoumakos, P. Karras, and N. Koziris. H2RDF+: High-performance distributed joins over large-scale RDF graphs. In X. Hu, T. Y. Lin, V. Raghavan, B. W. Wah, R. A. Baeza-Yates, G. Fox, C. Shahabi, M. Smith, Q. Yang, R. Ghani, W. Fan, R. Lempel, and R. Nambiar, Eds., *Proc. of the IEEE International Conference on Big Data*, pp. 255–263, October 6–9, Santa Clara, CA, 2013. DOI: 10.1109/BigData.2013.6691582 18, 29, 30, 31, 40, 49, 50, 59, 60, 65

N. Papailiou, D. Tsoumakos, I. Konstantinou, P. Karras, and N. Koziris. H2RDF+: An efficient data management system for big RDF graphs. In C. E. Dyreson, F. Li, and M. T. Özsu, Eds., *International Conference on Management of Data, SIGMOD*, pp. 909–912, ACM, Snowbird, UT, June 22–27, 2014. DOI: 10.1145/2588555.2594535 18

N. Papailiou, D. Tsoumakos, P. Karras, and N. Koziris. Graph-aware, workload-adaptive SPARQL query caching. In *Proc. of the ACM SIGMOD International Conference on Management of Data, SIGMOD'15*, pp. 1777–1792, 2015. DOI: 10.1145/2723372.2723714 65, 66

P. Peng, L. Zou, L. Chen, and D. Zhao. Query workload-based RDF graph fragmentation and allocation. In *Proc. of the 19th International Conference on Extending Database Technology, EDBT*, pp. 377–388, Bordeaux, France, March 15–16, OpenProceedings.org, 2016a. DOI: 10.5441/002/edbt.2016.35 37

P. Peng, L. Zou, M. T. Özsu, L. Chen, and D. Zhao. Processing SPARQL queries over distributed RDF graphs. *VLDB Journal*, 25(2):243–268, 2016b. DOI: 10.1007/s00778-015-0415-0 37, 40, 52, 53

M. Przyjaciel-Zablocki, A. Schätzle, T. Hornung, C. Dorner, and G. Lausen. Cascading map-side joins over HBase for scalable join processing. *CoRR*, abs/1206.6293, 2012. http://ar xiv.org/abs/1206.6293 31, 40, 50, 54, 55

R. Punnoose, A. Crainiceanu, and D. Rapp. Rya: A scalable RDF triple store for the clouds. In J. Darmont and T. B. Pedersen, Eds., *1st International Workshop on Cloud Intelligence (colocated with VLDB), Cloud-I'12*, p. 4, ACM, Istanbul, Turkey, August 31, 2012. DOI: 10.1145/2347673.2347677 30, 31, 40

G. Raschia, M. Theobald, and I. Manolescu. *Proc. of the 1st International Workshop on Open Data (WOD)*, 2012. 1

P. Ravindra, H. Kim, and K. Anyanwu. An intermediate algebra for optimizing RDF graph pattern matching on MapReduce. In G. Antoniou, M. Grobelnik, E. P. B. Simperl, B. Parsia, D. Plexousakis, P. D. Leenheer, and J. Z. Pan, Eds., *The Semantic Web: Research and Applications—8th Extended Semantic Web Conference, ESWC*, Heraklion, Crete, Greece, May 29–June 2, 2011, Proceedings, Part II, volume 6644 of *Lecture Notes in Computer Science*, pp. 46–61, Springer, 2011. DOI: 10.1007/978-3-642-21064-8_4 18, 26, 40, 44, 54, 55, 59, 60, 61, 66

RDF Concepts. RDF 1.1 concepts and abstract syntax. http://www.w3.org/TR/rdf11-concepts/, 2014. 5

K. Rohloff and R. E. Schantz. High-performance, massively scalable distributed systems using the MapReduce software framework: The SHARD triple-store. In E. Tilevich and P. Eugster, Eds., *SPLASH Workshop on Programming Support Innovations for Emerging Distributed Applications PSI EtA*, p. 4, ACM, Reno/Tahoe, Nevada, October 17, 2010. DOI: 10.1145/1940747.1940751 18, 25, 40, 44, 48

K. Rohloff and R. E. Schantz. Clause-iteration with MapReduce to scalably query datagraphs in the SHARD graph-store. In *4th International Workshop on Data-intensive Distributed Computing*, 2011. DOI: 10.1145/1996014.1996021 54, 55, 59, 66

S3. Amazon S3. http://aws.amazon.com/s3/, 2006. 13

S. Salihoglu and J. Widom. GPS: A graph processing system. In *Proc. of the 25th International Conference on Scientific and Statistical Database Management, SSDBM*, pp. 22:1–22:12, 2013. DOI: 10.1145/2484838.2484843 51

R. Sandberg, D. Goldberg, S. Kleiman, D. Walsh, and B. Lyon. Design and implementation of the Sun network file system. In *Proc. of the Summer USENIX Conference*, pp. 119–130, 1985. 13

A. Schätzle, M. Przyjaciel-Zablocki, and G. Lausen. PigSPARQL: Mapping SPARQL to pig Latin. In R. D. Virgilio, F. Giunchiglia, and L. Tanca, Eds., *Proc. of the International Workshop on Semantic Web Information Management, SWIM*, p. 4, ACM, Athens, Greece, June 12, 2011. DOI: 10.1145/1999299.1999303 18, 40, 54, 55

A. Schätzle, M. Przyjaciel-Zablocki, and G. Lausen. PigSPARQL: Mapping SPARQL to pig Latin. In *SWIM*, 2011. DOI: 10.1145/1999299.1999303 25, 44, 48

A. Schätzle, M. Przyjaciel-Zablocki, S. Skilevic, and G. Lausen. S2RDF: RDF querying with SPARQL on spark. *PVLDB*, 9(10):804–815, 2016. DOI: 10.14778/2977797.2977806 28, 40, 44

P. G. Selinger, M. M. Astrahan, D. D. Chamberlin, R. A. Lorie, and T. G. Price. Access path selection in a relational database management system. In P. A. Bernstein, Ed., *Proc. of the ACM SIGMOD International Conference on Management of Data*, pp. 23–34, ACM, Boston, MA, May 30–June 1, 1979. DOI: 10.1145/582095.582099 61, 65

B. Shao, H. Wang, and Y. Li. Trinity: A distributed graph engine on a memory cloud. In K. A. Ross, D. Srivastava, and D. Papadias, Eds., *Proc. of the ACM SIGMOD International Conference on Management of Data*, pp. 505–516, ACM, New York, June 22–27, 2013. DOI: 10.1145/2463676.2467799 32, 33, 38, 39, 40

SimpleDB. Amazon SimpleDB. http://aws.amazon.com/simpledb/, 2007. 14

I. Stanton and G. Kliot. Streaming graph partitioning for large distributed graphs. In *Proc. of the 18th ACM SIGKDD International Conference on Knowledge Discovery and Data Mining, KDD'12*, pp. 1222–1230, 2012. DOI: 10.1145/2339530.2339722 24

R. Stein and V. Zacharias. RDF on cloud number nine. In *NeFORS Workshop*, May 2010a. 50, 54, 55

R. Stein and V. Zacharias. RDF on cloud number nine. In *4th Workshop on New Forms of Reasoning for the Semantic Web: Scalable and Dynamic*, pp. 11–23, Citeseer, 2010b. 30, 31, 40

F. M. Suchanek, G. Kasneci, and G. Weikum. Yago: A core of semantic knowledge. In *WWW*, 2007. DOI: 10.1145/1242572.1242667 2

H. J. ter Horst. Completeness, decidability and complexity of entailment for RDF schema and a semantic extension involving the OWL vocabulary. *Web Semantics*, 3(2–3):79–115, 2005a. DOI: 10.1016/j.websem.2005.06.001 70, 71

H. J. ter Horst. Completeness, decidability and complexity of entailment for RDF schema and a semantic extension involving the OWL vocabulary. *Web Semantic*, 3(2–3):79–115, October 2005b. DOI: 10.1016/j.websem.2005.06.001 9

Y. Theoharis, V. Christophides, and G. Karvounarakis. Benchmarking database representations of RDF/S stores. In Y. Gil, E. Motta, V. R. Benjamins, and M. A. Musen, Eds., *The Semantic Web—ISWC, 4th International Semantic Web Conference, ISWC, Galway, Ireland, November 6–10, Proceedings*, volume 3729 of *Lecture Notes in Computer Science*, pp. 685–701, Springer, 2005. DOI: 10.1007/11574620_49 26

M. Thomazo. Compact rewritings for existential rules. In *IJCAI, Proc. of the 23rd International Joint Conference on Artificial Intelligence*, pp. 1125–1131, Beijing, China, August 3–9, 2013. http://www.aaai.org/ocs/index.php/IJCAI/IJCAI13/paper/view/6826 12

C. Tsourakakis, C. Gkantsidis, B. Radunovic, and M. Vojnovic. FENNEL: Streaming graph partitioning for massive scale graphs. In *Proc. of the 7th ACM International Conference on Web Search and Data Mining, WSDM'14*, pp. 333–342, 2014. DOI: 10.1145/2556195.2556213 24

O. Udrea, A. Pugliese, and V. S. Subrahmanian. GRIN: A graph based RDF index. In *Proc. of the 22nd National Conference on Artificial Intelligence—Volume 2, AAAI'07*, pp. 1465–1470, 2007. 2

J. Urbani, S. Kotoulas, E. Oren, and F. van Harmelen. Scalable distributed reasoning using MapReduce. In *ISWC*, 2009. DOI: 10.1007/978-3-642-04930-9_40 68, 69, 70, 72

J. Urbani, S. Kotoulas, J. Maassen, F. van Harmelen, and H. E. Bal. OWL reasoning with WebPIE: Calculating the closure of 100 billion triples. In *ESWC*, pp. 213–227, 2010. DOI: 10.1007/978-3-642-13486-9_15 70, 72

J. Urbani, F. van Harmelen, S. Schlobach, and H. Bal. QueryPIE: Backward reasoning for OWL horst over very large knowledge bases. In *ISWC*, 2011a. DOI: 10.1007/978-3-642-25073-6_46 71, 72

J. Urbani, F. van Harmelen, S. Schlobach, and H. E. Bal. QueryPIE: Backward reasoning for OWL horst over very large knowledge bases. In L. Aroyo, C. Welty, H. Alani, J. Taylor, A. Bernstein, L. Kagal, N. F. Noy, and E. Blomqvist, Eds., *The Semantic Web—ISWC—10th International Semantic Web Conference, Proceedings, Part I*, Bonn, Germany, October 23–27, volume 7031 of *Lecture Notes in Computer Science*, pp. 730–745, Springer, 2011b. DOI: 10.1007/978-3-642-25073-6_46 12

J. Urbani, S. Kotoulas, J. Maassen, F. van Harmelen, and H. E. Bal. WebPIE: A web-scale parallel inference engine using MapReduce. *Journal of Web Semantic*, 10:59–75, 2012. DOI: 10.1016/j.websem.2011.05.004 68, 69

J. Urbani, A. Margara, C. J. H. Jacobs, F. van Harmelen, and H. E. Bal. Dynamite: Parallel materialization of dynamic RDF data. In H. Alani, L. Kagal, A. Fokoue, P. T. Groth, C. Biemann, J. X. Parreira, L. Aroyo, N. F. Noy, C. Welty, and K. Janowicz, Eds., *The Semantic Web—ISWC—12th International Semantic Web Conference, Proceedings, Part I*, Sydney, NSW, Australia, October 21–25, volume 8218 of *Lecture Notes in Computer Science*, pp. 657–672, Springer, 2013. DOI: 10.1007/978-3-642-41335-3_41 12

L. G. Valiant. A bridging model for parallel computation. *Communications of the ACM*, 33(8):103–111, August 1990. DOI: 10.1145/79173.79181 53

R. D. Virgilio. Distributed in-memory SPARQL processing via DOF analysis. In V. Markl, S. Orlando, B. Mitschang, P. Andritsos, K. Sattler, and S. Breß, Eds., *Proc. of the 20th International Conference on Extending Database Technology, EDBT*, Venice, Italy, March 21–24, pp. 234–245, OpenProceedings.org, 2017. DOI: 10.5441/002/edbt.2017.22 38, 40, 47, 51, 64, 66

W3C. Resource description framework (RDF): Concepts and abstract syntax. `http://www.w3.org/TR/2004/REC-rdf-concepts-20040210/`, 2004. 1

W3C. SPARQL query language for RDF. `http://www.w3.org/TR/rdf-sparql-query/`, 2008. 10

W3C. SPARQL 1.1 query language for RDF. `http://www.w3.org/TR/sparql11-query/`, 2013. 1, 10

W3C. RDF 1.1 semantics. `http://www.w3.org/TR/rdf11-mt/`, 2014a. 8, 69

W3C. RDF schema 1.1. `http://www.w3.org/TR/rdf-schema/`, 2014b. 1, 7

W3C OWL Working Group. OWL 2 Web Ontology Language Document Overview (Second Edition). W3C Recommendation, `https://www.w3.org/TR/owl2-overview/`, 2012. 1

G. Wang and C. Chan. Multi-query optimization in MapReduce framework. *PVLDB*, 7(3):145–156, 2013. DOI: 10.14778/2732232.2732234 74

J. Weaver and J. A. Hendler. Parallel materialization of the finite RDFS closure for hundreds of millions of triples. In A. Bernstein, D. R. Karger, T. Heath, L. Feigenbaum, D. Maynard, E. Motta, and K. Thirunarayan, Eds., *The Semantic Web—ISWC, 8th International Semantic Web Conference, Proceedings*, Chantilly, VA, October 25–29, volume 5823 of *Lecture Notes in Computer Science*, pp. 682–697, Springer, 2009. DOI: 10.1007/978-3-642-04930-9_43 69, 72

C. Weiss, P. Karras, and A. Bernstein. Hexastore: Sextuple indexing for semantic web data management. *PVLDB*, 1(1):1008–1019, 2008a. `http://www.vldb.org/pvldb/1/1453965.pdf` DOI: 10.14778/1453856.1453965 29

C. Weiss, P. Karras, and A. Bernstein. Hexastore: Sextuple indexing for semantic web data management. *PVLDB*, 1(1):1008–1019, 2008b. DOI: 10.14778/1453856.1453965 2

K. Wilkinson, C. Sayers, H. A. Kuno, and D. Raynolds. Efficient RDF storage and retrieval in Jena2. In *SWDB (in conjunction with VLDB)*, 2003. 2

B. Wu, H. Jin, and P. Yuan. Scalable SAPRQL querying processing on large RDF data in cloud computing environment. In *ICPCA/SWS*, 2012. DOI: 10.1007/978-3-642-37015-1_55 37

B. Wu, Y. Zhou, P. Yuan, L. Liu, and H. Jin. Scalable SPARQL querying using path parti-
tioning. In J. Gehrke, W. Lehner, K. Shim, S. K. Cha, and G. M. Lohman, Eds., *31st IEEE
International Conference on Data Engineering, ICDE*, pp. 795–806, Computer Society, Seoul,
South Korea, April 13–17, 2015. DOI: 10.1109/ICDE.2015.7113334 18, 34, 36, 40

B. Wu, Y. Zhou, H. Jin, and A. Deshpande. Parallel SPARQL query optimization. In *33rd
IEEE International Conference on Data Engineering, ICDE*, pp. 547–558, Computer Society,
San Diego, CA, April 19–22, 2017. DOI: 10.1109/ICDE.2017.110 64, 66

M. Zaharia, M. Chowdhury, M. J. Franklin, S. Shenker, and I. Stoica. Spark: Cluster
computing with working sets. In E. M. Nahum and D. Xu, Eds., *2nd USENIX Workshop on Hot Topics in Cloud Computing, HotCloud'10*, USENIX Association, Boston, MA,
June 22, 2010. `https://www.usenix.org/conference/hotcloud-10/spark-cluster-
computing-working-sets` 18

M. Zaharia, M. Chowdhury, T. Das, A. Dave, J. Ma, M. McCauley, M. J. Franklin, S.
Shenker, and I. Stoica. Resilient distributed datasets: A fault-tolerant abstraction for in-
memory cluster computing. In *Proc. of the 9th USENIX Conference on Networked Systems
Design and Implementation, NSDI'12*, pp. 2–2, USENIX Association, Berkeley, CA, 2012.
`http://dl.acm.org/citation.cfm?id=2228298.2228301` 18

K. Zeng, J. Yang, H. Wang, B. Shao, and Z. Wang. A distributed graph engine for web scale
RDF data. *PVLDB*, 6(4):265–276, 2013. `http://www.vldb.org/pvldb/vol6/p265-zeng
.pdf` DOI: 10.14778/2535570.2488333 51, 54, 55, 65

X. Zhang, L. Chen, and M. Wang. Towards efficient join processing over large RDF graph
using MapReduce. In *SSDBM*, 2012. DOI: 10.1007/978-3-642-31235-9_16 26, 40, 44, 50,
54, 55

X. Zhang, L. Chen, Y. Tong, and M. Wang. EAGRE: Towards scalable I/O efficient SPARQL
query evaluation on the cloud. In *ICDE*, 2013. DOI: 10.1109/icde.2013.6544856 28, 40,
45, 54, 55

L. Zou, J. Mo, L. Chen, M. T. Özsu, and D. Zhao. gStore: Answering SPARQL queries via
subgraph matching. *PVLDB*, 4(8):482–493, 2011. `http://www.vldb.org/pvldb/vol4/
p482-zou.pdf` DOI: 10.14778/2002974.2002976 37

L. Zou, M. T. Özsu, L. Chen, X. Shen, R. Huang, and D. Zhao. gStore: A graph-based
SPARQL query engine. *VLDB Journal*, 23(4):565–590, 2014. DOI: 10.1007/s00778-013-
0337-7 2

Authors' Biographies

ZOI KAOUDI

Zoi Kaoudi is a Senior Researcher in the DIMA group at the Technische Universität Berlin (TUB). She has previously worked as a Scientist in the Qatar Computing Research Institute (QCRI) of the Hamad Bin Khalifa University in Qatar, in IMIS-Athena Research Center as a research associate, and Inria as a postdoctoral researcher. She received her Ph.D. from the National and Kapodistrian University of Athens in 2011. Her research interests include cross-platform data processing, machine learning systems, and distributed RDF query processing and reasoning. Recently she has been the proceedings chair of EDBT 2019, co-chaired the TKDE poster track co-located with ICDE 2018, and co-organized the MLDAS 2019 held in Qatar. She has co-authored articles in both database and Semantic Web communities and served as a member of a Program Committee for several international database conferences.

IOANA MANOLESCU

Ioana Manolescu is a senior Inria researcher, and the lead of the CEDAR team (joint between Inria Saclay and the LIX lab of École polytechnique) in France. The CEDAR team research focuses on rich data analytics at cloud scale. Ioana is a member of the PVLDB Endowment Board of Trustees and has served for four years (including as president) of the ACM SIGMOD Jim Gray Ph.D. dissertation committee. Recently, she has been a general chair of the IEEE ICDE 2018 conference, an associate editor for *PVLDB* 2017 and 2018, and the program chair of SSDBBM 2016. She has co-authored more than 130 articles in international journals and conferences, and contributed to several books. Her main research interests include data models and algorithms for computational fact-checking, performance optimizations for semistructured data and the Semantic Web, and distributed architectures for complex large data.

STAMATIS ZAMPETAKIS

Stamatis Zampetakis is an R&D engineer at TIBCO Orchestra Networks and a PMC member of Apache Calcite. Previously, he was a postdoctoral researcher at Inria, from where he also received his Ph.D. in 2015. Before that, he worked in FORTH-ICS as a research assistant. His research interests are in the broad area of query optimization with emphasis on RDF query processing and visualization.

Printed in the United States
by Baker & Taylor Publisher Services